Praise for *Flirting with Finance*

"Fascinating! *Flirting with Finance* is cleverly disguised as a romance novel. I love it! I'm probably very typical because I was taught nothing about finances as a little girl."

— Toni Andrews
"So Many Books" on PBS

"I love the way you put it, you make it seem so easy."

— Marybel Rodriguez
"The Balancing Act" on Lifetime

"Beck's book combines fiction with reality in a nod to a life many young women are fantasizing about while mixing in a dose of financial education."

— Judy Martel
Bankrate.com

"Everyone in the hospitality industry should read this book! When can you read a romance novel with all this practical information on handling your own finances from your first checking account to knowing what is a hedge fund? I am giving a copy to all my staff."

— Thomas A. Kershaw
Owner of Hampshire House Corporation
Operator of the *Cheers* bars in Beacon Hill
& Faneuil Hall Marketplace in Boston

"*Flirting with Finance* will leave the reader with an emotional state of empowerment."

— Tim Goering,
President, Seaside Bank & Trust

Flirting With Finance

✦

An Easy Way To Learn
Life's Financial Lessons

Gwendolyn Beck
with Kathleen Pickering

iUniverse, Inc.
Bloomington

Flirting With Finance
An Easy Way To Learn Life's Financial Lessons

iUniverse books may be ordered through booksellers or by contacting:

iUniverse
1663 Liberty Drive
Bloomington, IN 47403
www.iuniverse.com
1-800-Authors (1-800-288-4677)

ISBN: 978-0-595-51076-4 (sc)
ISBN: 978-0-595-50275-2 (hc)
ISBN: 978-0-595-61757-9 (e)

Printed in the United States of America

iUniverse rev. date: 12/10/2012

To my Mother, Yvonne Bixby,
And all the brave, strong women who lost
their battle with breast cancer.

Here is the deepest secret nobody knows,
Here is the root of the root,
And the bud of the bud,
And the sky of the sky of a tree called life
Which grows higher than the soul can hope or the mind can hide

I carry your heart,
I carry it in my heart.

— E.E. Cummings

Flirting with Finance

Author's Note

The economy is constantly changing and economic events today will probably be completely different from events a year from now. It's very important to be flexible and cautious with your investments and major purchases. This book teaches the basics of finance and will get you through any situation, because the basics really never change. People, both smart and not so smart, will try to convince you this time it's different—it's not. Remember, no one knows everything. So, as long as you know the basics, and recognize that what sounds too good to be true is too good to be true, you'll get the results you want. We all make mistakes—that's okay. Just keep going forward.

This book will teach you the principles of investing that will get you through any economic environment. During my career, I've seen the economy roll through many ups and downs. I worked on the bond trading floor at Credit Suisse in taxable fixed income on the U.S. government securities desk. I started as junior-assistant flunkie, passed my series 7 and 63 and left when the bond market burst in the mid-nineties. But, I did learn an enormous amount about finance and how the system works. Seeking a better environment, I moved to Morgan Stanley and the world of stocks, retirement accounts, and financial planning. I hit pay dirt on the ground level of the IPO boom and enjoyed the ride until that boom came crashing down in 2001.

After the crash, I continued to work as a Financial Advisor because I like to help people. And, finance is a big part of everyone's life! I really believe if you can get your finances in order the rest of your life will fall into place. So, I went in search of a fun, easy-to-read financial book to help my clients and friends. Couldn't find one! So, went in search of an awesome romance writer - found one—and "Flirting with Finance" is the result.

In "Flirting with Finance" we follow the life of Samantha Davis as she goes through the ups and downs of love, finance and life—they are intertwined after all. It's a romance book that will teach you about finance along the way, because that's how life works. Some things you'll learn without realizing you just learned them! And, although Samantha is a fictitious character, all her stories are true, and the finance is accurate (unless they change the laws after publication). After you finish reading, keep this book for reference purposes—your financial life will constantly be growing and shrinking and this book has valuable information to help you adjust to the changing environment.

"Be smart with your money, make it work for you!"

– Gwendolyn Beck

Forward

My name is Samantha Davis. I'm here to tell you about how my love affair with money started. Not a fling. Not a cash-to-the-wind romance, but a strong, interest-growing, satisfying love affair with my funds. It was rocky at first, changing my desires, and going without shiny new things. It was celibacy with cash as I refused temptation by walking away from the lust of the purchase.

Well, hold on. My finance attraction is not quite a love affair. Honestly, it's a full blown addiction. Yes, I did say, addiction. I'm addicted to finance. Not shopping. Not chocolate ... well, maybe chocolate. Not drugs. Not liquor. Not shoes ... well, maybe shoes. But, I am definitely and most undeniably, addicted to my financial well being. I have been for years now, and nothing you say or do can stop me. I love my financial freedom!

There, I said it.

And not a hair fell out of place.

My palms aren't sweaty.

The gloss isn't chewed off my lips.

That's because I understand my money, how to use it and how to have it work for me!

Don't get me wrong. I didn't start out this way. This blond haired, blue eyed, girl-next-door flirted her way into financial disaster before realizing money, like love, has a language all its own ... a language few people understand.

I was slow to realize the obsession of financial freedom. Now, like breathing, I can meet your gaze and confess my addiction with pride. I get to keep and cultivate my growing portfolio, and if I want a Mercedes Benz or Giuseppe Zanotti shoes I know how to buy them. I'm passionate about the results of my investments because I made so many foolish mistakes along the way. Just like love, sometimes we learn the hard way, but when we make sound emotional and financial decisions both our dividends and personal security multiply. Learning the hard way to appreciate all commitments makes them that much sweeter once they are achieved!

The rock-bottom financial blunders I made changed me from finance flirt to finance addict. I'm here to share my blunders with you. I want to help you because I never want financial ignorance, no matter how blissful, to stand between you, your happiness, and your financial independence. I learned the hard way. I want you to understand, loud and clear, that a financially educated person is an asset to herself and her world.

Besides, sound finances feel soooooo good.

Just thinking about it sends shivers up my spine.

So, I'd love to begin my story with "once upon a time," but, well, this is no fairy tale. It's real life. My education started in my last year of high school. My father, as the man of the house, considered the family's financial well-being his concern. Mom was happy to let him run the show. She believed Dad made life easier by handling the finances—less to think about, and all. Wasn't that what most women wanted?

Mom discovered she was so very wrong.

Dad died just after I graduated from high school. Through my own sadness, I watched my mother grieve the loss of her life partner only to discover she'd become trapped in the financial maze of her existence. She understood basic check writing and bill paying, but Dad's stock and bond investments, insurance, numerous cars and retirement plans terrified her. Settling my father's estate practically drove my mother to drink … heavily. She slowly climbed out of financial ignorance while never quite trusting herself with financial responsibility. I decided never to let that happen to me.

But, I was a slow learner! Life and love were about to rain down upon me in spades and my financial umbrella was riddled with emotional holes. Since I wish a far better fate for you, here is the story of my life, my loves, the mistakes I've made, the places I've lived, my children and my finances. So, let's go back to the beginning.

My first taste of finance came with a passbook savings account my father had opened for me to stash babysitting and birthday money. How was I to know my $2000 languished under the paltry 0.5% the account offered? I didn't understand the whole banking process until I left for college and opened my first checking account.

As I said, my finance obsession was slow to grow. Not knowing the next move to make or what questions to ask pulled me two steps back for every step forward. My father had the foresight to budget for college years, but it wasn't enough to pay for an out-of-state university. So, to make tuition payments easier on my mother, I chose a state college near my home town. No sooner was I settled in the dorm, with a roommate named Parker, who would prove to be the best friend a girl could have, when I headed to the nearest bank to open my first checking account.

A small thrill ran through me when I saw the teller lines. Finance in action. I loved it. I could practically smell currency in the air. The officious looking managers sitting at desks along the wall looked so darned capable. I waited for the next account manager like the rest of America about to embark on financial independence. I liked the sensation … the tingle right down to the tips of my fingers.

I imagined myself so wealthy some day that I'd be a revered philanthropist. Cities would name streets and libraries after me, Samantha Davis. The media would know me by my first name. Like Madonna or Donald or Beyonce—SamDee would roll of their tongues.

A sigh escaped my lips. I should get a grip. I was opening a checking account with my $2000 passbook and a matching check from Mom, not saving the world. Still, I wondered if relinquishing my money would hurt me or set me free. I had to come to terms with the fact that

I was a checking account virgin. My mouth grew dry at the prospect of revealing this truth to the all-knowing account manager.

Then he said, "Can I help you, Miss?"

The pale, young man motioned me to a chair. A tad giddy, I sat my size four body into the overstuffed chair.

I met his gaze with authority. "I need a checking account."

He slid a form under his hand. "What type of checking account would you like?"

Was he kidding? I chuckled, saying, "Well, one with checks, of course."

He grinned. "Have you banked with us before?"

I swallowed hard and leaned closer. With what I hoped were puppy-dog eyes, I shared my secret. "I've never opened an account anywhere before. You are my first."

His gaze fell to my lips as if he wanted to kiss me. He cleared his throat. "Well, miss. *We have a CAP account, a Crown account, a regular account, free checking and money market checks. A lot depends on how much money you're going to deposit and how many checks you need to write each month."* He held up a slender finger. *"And, whether or not you want to deposit securities."*

I felt my nose wrinkle. *"Securities?"*

I think this is when he realized I knew nothing about banking. His gaze softened. I'd swear he felt tempted to take my hand in his. He said, *"Stocks and bonds. Would you like me to explain them?"*

Whoa! Way too much financial information at one time. I wasn't ready yet. I wiped away perspiration beading on my upper lip. I inhaled a slow, steady breath. "For now, why don't we just discuss checking accounts?"

It took a while to explain the different checking accounts, but I eventually understood. I sighed with relief that we were discussing checking accounts and not stocks and bonds—yet. My crash course in those, however, was coming sooner than I imagined. It never occurred to me that banks and investment houses would pay me to keep my money with them. But for now, here's the breakdown of what the account manager said.

CHECKING ACCOUNTS:

"There are many types of checking accounts. Picking the correct account is very important in basic money management. If you're smart about managing all facets of the money you make, you can make your money work for you; and thereby, have extra money for manicures, pedicures, groceries—all the important stuff."

(By the flush in his cheeks when he said, 'pedicures', I think he was flirting with me.)

He continued. *"First rule to remember: Banks (Bank of America, Wells Fargo, Citibank, etc.) and investment houses (UBS, Schwab, TD AmeriTrade, Morgan Stanley, etc.) will pay you to keep your money with them. Sometimes there is a minimum deposit, but it's always important to try not to pay the fees, because they'll eat into your money. The fees sound small, but if you add them up they can become quite large. For example, if you pay $10 per month for checking its $120 per year (lots of manicures), $8 is $96, etc. So, the goal is to not pay anything. Remember: if you can make your money work for you at all levels, even the smallest ones, your money will grow."*

I followed that. Did you? If not, take the time to read the section again. It's worth the adrenaline rush when the facts make sense.

Next, the account manager explained the differences between banks and investment houses:

"When it comes to simple checking accounts, the primary difference between a bank and an investment house is that banks can accept cash as a deposit and investment houses cannot. If you can manage your cash through an ATM (automatic teller machine) a checking account at an investment house might be a better way to go, because they typically will pay you more. They also have bill pay options available."

Okay, now pay attention here. Once you understand this information, you'll start to feel satisfaction flow through you like brandy. Feel the addiction slowly take affect!

All banks and investment houses have brochures describing the different types of accounts they offer and all call them by a name chosen by their marketing departments, but GENERALLY THESE ARE THE CATEGORIES:

FREE CHECKING: (Of course, it's only free if you follow their rules.) Usually requires direct deposit, i.e., your pay check goes directly into your account on a regular basis. You still have to buy the checks and if the requirements aren't met you get charged a monthly fee. For example, one bank (we won't name names) charges approximately $5.95 per month or $71.40 a year ($71.40 is not 'free'). Another's free checking is the cost to print the checks or $1. (So, even it's not really free.) Do research in your hometown to find the best banks, and don't let the salespeople pressure or intimidate you! Sometimes, banks will offer specials that are advertised in the local newspaper—take advantage of them! And, never hesitate to move your account if you're not happy. If you eventually work for a large company, be sure to take advantage of ALL programs offered, i.e. credit unions, special deals, etc., they have purchasing power and usually negotiate better deals.

REGULAR CHECKING: Usually this type of account will require a minimum balance (which varies by bank) and you still have to buy checks. The fee is higher if you miss the minimum; one bank charges $11 per month with direct deposit and $12 per month without. That's $144 per year—for me, six (6) months of manicures!

PREMIUM BANKING: Usually some clever name like PREMIUM, CROWN OR ADVANTAGE, it requires a substantial daily balance, $1,000 to $10,000 depending on the bank, but offers additional services. If your balance falls below the minimum, charges can be up to $20 per month or a whopping $240 per year. Yikes!

I'm going to have to be really careful to avoid paying extra fees. Grandpa Wallace told me to always ask the bank, especially smaller banks, to waive fees—actually he said to ask everyone for a discount on everything! Great idea, especially since I always need manicure money. I kept his advice in mind as the account manager explained how interest rates work.

INTEREST RATES—or How to Make Money on Your Money! Banks will pay you money, fondly known as interest, on the money you keep with them. When you deposit your money, you are in effect loaning the bank your money. They in turn loan it out to people for homes, cars, etc., and to small business to meet their expenses. The banks will pay you *depending on what type of account you have and how much money is in that account. Banks will also offer specials to get you to move your money to them. For example: if you are paid 2.5% on $1,000 you will make $25 per year—doesn't sound like much, but trust me, it adds up.*

TIP: If you have $2500 or more, check the interest rates very carefully. Take the time to do the math. Money here means only one thing—more for you later!!!

ACCOUNTS THAT OFFER MONEY MARKET SWEEPS AND HOLD SECURITIES: These accounts are designed to hold cash and securities (stocks, bonds, mutual funds, etc.—more on those later), and offer "sweeps" for your cash on a daily basis. In other words, all cash is swept into a money market account (an account that pays interest) on a daily basis. But, be careful, most banks charge for the sweep option, some as high as 30 basis points (more on basis points later, but it is 0.30 %; again, doesn't sound like much, but it adds up).

ONLINE BANKING is a great way to go if you've mastered avoiding hackers. Please make sure your password is complicated and change it often, and don't access your account on an open connection. Most banks charge no fee for this service.

That was a mouthful. No? How did you do? Again, re-read any of the information until it's clear. I promise you, you'll love me for it!

TIP: Always check on-line and in the newspapers for specials. Banks and brokerage houses are very competitive and they always offer specials!

BE SURE TO READ THE SMALL PRINT. HIDDEN FEES WILL COST YOU.

REMEMBER: SAVINGS ACCOUNTS ARE FOR CHILDREN. IT'S TIME TO UPGRADE YOUR MONEY.

Now, this next section *'balancing the checkbook'* is crucial to all budding finance addicts. Believe me when I say, I learned the hard way. Even after my fair-haired account manager explained checkbook maintenance, I still had trouble. I kept thinking the balance I had was greater than the checks I was writing because the previous checks hadn't cleared. So, my checks turned to rubber … ahem … started bouncing! How embarrassing was that?! So pay close attention here. It's really easy to understand.

HOW TO BALANCE A CHECKBOOK: this is really important because it costs a lot in fees if you mess up and bounce a check. Remember, just because you have checks doesn't mean you have money. You'll be given a check ledger/register when you receive your new checks, write in how much you deposited in the credit side. Then each check you write put the amount in the payment or debit side. Add the credit side and subtract the debit side. Be sure to keep up with the money you're spending on your check card and cash withdrawals from ATMs, too. (See the Basic Check Register and the Check Codes in Appendix A.) Unfortunately, you'll have to do the math yourself, but now most smart phones have calculators in them, so be sure to keep up. For more on this topic see Appendix A. On-line bill pay is an excellent way to go as it gives you up to date balances of your account. But, watch your money and make sure you don't get hacked—wouldn't want to lose any! And, NEVER click on an email link which was emailed to you from what appears to be a bank—this is a favorite 'phishing' move of hackers.

Did you get all that? It makes sense. I have to admit, listening to the account manager explain my choices, made understanding this concept much easier. He needed my driver's license, social security number, date of birth, family names, place of birth, credit checks, and first born. (Just kidding. Wanted to see if you were paying attention.)

They had a special Free Checking for Students which I chose. When I land a corporate job, I will switch to Free Checking with Direct Deposit (of course, it's only free if I follow the specific rules). The direct deposit will be perfect because I wouldn't have to handle a pay check.

Also, *my checking account comes with a check card, which works like a debit card (ATM card). A debit card takes money directly out of your account every time you use it, and you must deduct the amount from your account as you would a written check.*

A credit card? I didn't dare. I'd stick to my check book and ATM card for now.

1

College was so much fun—the parties, new friends and being on my own. I studied my tail off and worked part-time as a waitress. Now, at the ripe age of twenty-two, I graduated and headed to the big city. My roommate, Parker and I found a great studio apartment which we dubbed the "Hallway", because the extra-long hallway was the most striking feature of our postage-stamp living space. We loved it! My raven-haired friend's talent and charm landed her a job as sous-chef at a very expensive restaurant in New York. I landed a paralegal position with a top-notch law firm. And, best of all, I had met Alan just before I graduated.

I fell in love at first sight.

Alan Abercrombie is one of those blond, blue eyed, angel-faced hunky types. Success glows like a halo around his splendid, thirty year old head. Yes, he is slightly older, but we look great together. (There, I said it!) His job as a TFI bond trader at Credit Suisse made him a financial genius compared to my then-gross-ineptitude. Actually, my crush on him was so complete I didn't even bother to discover what a TFI bond trader did until it was too late.

Major mistake number one!

I should have asked more questions when he told me about his job on our first date. We were lazing on a beach blanket with Parker and her boyfriend. The lull in the conversation made me squirm while Alan's gaze followed my hand trailing sunscreen across my belly. To distract him, I asked, "What do you do?"

He said, "About what?"

"You know. A typical day at work."

His eyes fell on the sequined pineapples adorning the top of my draw-string bikini (my best summer investment!) before his gaze took on a far-away look. He got so excited about describing his job, he was oblivious to the fact his fingers stroked the inside of my arm, sending goose-bumps from my wrist to my ankles.

I should have paid attention to his words, not the havoc his fingers were wreaking!

He said, "I get up at 5:30 and leave the house by 6:15. Take a cab from Tribeca and arrive at Credit Suisse Headquarters around 6:45. Grab a cup of coffee, four newspapers and am seated in my chair by 7:15. *Then, I read the papers and the morning research.*"

Research. Okay, now I could grab onto that word. Glancing over the rim of my sunglasses, I asked, "What's *morning research?*"

He rolled from his belly to lie on his side, facing me. The way his lips moved when he spoke made concentrating difficult. *"It's a daily update on what's going on in the world that could affect the bond markets. It varies depending on what economic numbers are coming out and what the Strategist has to say. Remember, as land of the rising sun, Asia starts the day, and then Europe opens, and as the earth spins on its axis, we open last."*

I was thinking, "Huh?" But instead, I handed him the sunscreen.

He smeared some on his nose, saying, *"I listen to what's happening with the futures market in Chicago and then, depending upon which economic numbers come out or random news I hear, my day takes off. Normally though all hell breaks loose around 8:30 with 550 traders and salespeople yelling orders back and forth. And, I mean yelling, as loud as they possibly can! They actually fired one girl because her voice didn't carry far enough. I sit wedged among twelve computer screens and 120 phone lines. My right hand is doing one thing while the left hand, something else. It's managed chaos at the speed of light!"*

Now, I was too plain embarrassed to show my ignorance. I closed my dropped jaw by saying, "I'd lose my mind." That might not have been the right response because he frowned and blinked a couple of times.

He said, "Sam, it's hellish, but the most exciting career I could ever imagine."

Minor blunder on my part, but I think he forgave me because of my bikini.

My first major blunder with Alan came the first night I moved into the city. The doorman announced Alan was in the lobby while I was still catching my breath from arriving late and chatting up our new digs with Parker. Still in jeans and sweaty from lugging my suitcase through the simmering city, I dashed through a cloud of talc and perfume, touched up my makeup and hopped into a sundress. Knowing how punctual he was, I felt awful for making him wait thirty minutes. I wiped my sweaty palms on my sundress as the elevator doors opened.

Alan looked good enough to eat. A grin creased his lips as he reached for my hand.

"Samantha, you're gorgeous. I've missed you!"

I pirouetted once for him before his strong arms pulled me close. I enjoyed a heart-stopping, knee-melting kiss as delicious for me as it was for anyone watching.

Then, like a complete idiot basking in the gaze of those beautiful blue eyes I said, "So how was your day? The Internet said the market was up 240 points."

Mr. Wonderful looked like he took a bullet. He needed a moment to recover, while I thought his breathlessness was from the low cleavage of my dress. He finally kissed me on the forehead and said, "You're sweet to ask, Sam, but I'm a bond trader."

Still unaware I had said anything wrong I took his arm and let him lead me off to a dinner I was sure would be divine. While I thought I had asked a question dripping with innuendo that I cared, in reality I had said, don't let this little confection of a dress fool you.

Behind these baby blues is a brain that doesn't know the difference between a stock and a bond!

Alan is no slacker. I lost points, big time.

2

Monday was my first day at work. The receptionist directed me to a conference room for Orientation. A polished, power-exuding woman entered the room. Her gold, name-tag read, Penny Pincher.

I laughed out loud, only to discover it wasn't a joke.

Poised, with a beautiful smile, she said,

"Hello, and welcome to Nottingham, McCabe & Juroe. We're very happy you're part of our firm now. *This Orientation is designed to familiarize you with policies and procedures and also to explain your benefits.*"

She motioned to the folders on our desks. Now, this section is important, my friend. Anyone joining the working world must know this information. Here is what she said:

"The first form is a W-4 form. This is an Employee's Withholding Allowance Certificate. On this form you must claim the number of dependents you have. It also requires your address. This is the address of your residence, not your parents' or grandparents' house. We also need your social security number. The social security number is for payroll purposes only and will not be given to anyone else.

"The second form is an I-9 form which verifies your employment eligibility and states that you are who you are. In other words, a

declaration of citizenship. Of course, we'll need proof positive that you are eligible to work in the United States, so pull out your passport, birth certificate or pertinent documents. Medical insurance will start two months after your hire date. The options for different plans with their corresponding prices are listed in the folder you received on your desk."

I shuffled through the folder in front of me.

I'd filled out a W-4 form once before when I worked at the restaurant, but, the section regarding claiming dependents confused me.

Ms. Pincher continued.

"You will also be eligible for our 401(k) retirement plan in two months. There will be a separate meeting to explain those options to you. For now, please fill out, sign and date the W-4 form and the I-9 form, and pass those forward with your passport or green card."

My passport? I never had a passport. Besides, I'm an American. Did they need a passport from me? I raised my hand and asked.

She said, *"The Patriot Act, passed after 9/11, demands that everyone prove they are eligible to work in the United States. Your driver's license and social security number are no longer enough."*

Ms. Pincher just happened to have passport applications. I could have my photo taken in personnel, and for the government fee of $110, I could have a passport in several weeks. A passport would be handy. I just read an article in 'Cosmo' about a woman who always went to lunch with her passport and bikini in her purse, because she never knew when adventure might arrive.

I turned my attention to the W-4 form. Heaven knows small print was intended to challenge one's concentration, but my withholding depended on my understanding of this information.

Was I my own dependent? An independent woman should know these answers.

Penny Pincher didn't even blink as she explained I'd only claim myself because I would pay taxes on the amount that I earn. If you're married, how many deductions you claim would depend on how you file your income tax returns, whether it's jointly or separately.

So here are the links to the W-4 and the I-9 forms.
http://www.irs.gov/pub/irs-pdf/fw4.pdf
http://www.uscis.gov/files/form/i-9.pdf

If you've never seen these forms before, search them on the Internet and just take your time reading. Soon, they'll make sense. This new language will woo you. You'll begin to feel invincible understanding finance. You'll find yourself craving more. You're getting the bug! Bwa-haaa-haaa!

3

My first paycheck shocked me. My humongous salary had been reduced to a pittance. Sure, everyone said New York City taxes were high, but without so much as a wham-bam-thank you-ma'am, 40 percent of my income had been nipped. How would I pay rent and buy that gorgeous dress and shoes for my date with Alan tomorrow night?

I had no choice. I would simply have to open a Bloomingdale's account and charge the outfit. After all, Alan mentioned meeting his parents for the Thanksgiving holiday. I sensed commitment on the horizon. I had to take drastic measures.

Have you ever noticed when you're making a wrong decision, some little voice pops into your head as warning? The voice of reason for me became Grandpa Wallace. His voice echoed, "No debt! Only live off what you earn!"

Of course, his sage advice conflicted with my raw desire to look beautiful for Alan. I slapped an imaginary hand over Grandpa Wallace's mouth. Alan was far more important than accruing a smidgeon of debt.

I tossed my paycheck into the drawer. A girl had to do what a girl had to do.

Mistake number two.

Each time I opened the drawer those little details along the bottom of my paycheck harassed me. I finally took the paltry stipend from the drawer and examined it closer. What did FICA mean, anyway? Why did they take $80.42 for city tax and $185.52 for state tax? And, $677.08 for Federal tax—were they kidding? Medicare, I understood, only $39.27, but Social Security irritated like a bad thong: $167.97! I am only twenty two years old for heaven's sake! That left me with $1,558.07 net and rent alone costs me $1,050 per month. Did the government really get almost half my money for taxes?

So, let's see …

WHAT'S REALLY GOING ON IN A PAY CHECK:

- *Earnings, Regular Earnings or Gross Pay all mean the same thing: how much you made in that pay period.*
- *Federal Tax or Federal Withholding is the amount that goes to the Federal Government and is used for services such as the armed forces, highways, FBI, CIA, etc. This amount is determined as a percentage of your total expected yearly earnings and the number of deductions you claimed on your W-4 form.*
- *Social Security Tax, or in some cases OASDI Tax (Old Age, Survivors and Disability Insurance), is a government fund used to help people during their retirement. The good news is: our time will come and you can collect too.*
- *Medicare is a federal health program for people over 65; everyone pays in when they are young and reaps the benefits when they're older.*
- *FICA, Federal Insurance Contributions Act tax (okay, pay attention here) is a combination of a 6.2% social security tax and a 1.45% Medicare tax. The social security tax is assessed on wages up to $87,000; the Medicare tax is assessed on all wages.*
- *State and City Taxes can be steep depending on where you live, and, are used to pay for infrastructure such as water and sewer, schools, roads and the ever helpful State Troopers.*

- *Net Pay: you get to keep this. Remember. Don't spend it all in one place.*

And, next month, I'll have to pay $138.03 for medical and dental insurance. I needed a latte. A hot bath. Anything to relieve the knot rising in my chest. I wished my tiny salary would stop staring back at me. So, what if that Stella McCartney dress and Jimmy Choo shoes cost $1269 of my $1558.07 income? My career promised plenty of paychecks ahead. The money would come. I was sure of it.

I burst into the apartment, new outfit in tow. Parker's eyes lit up when they fell on the clothes. She gushed over my hot dress. I know she intended to compliment me when she said I'd look good in a burlap bag and didn't need to spend exorbitant amounts of money on clothes. But, my guilt alarm shrilled when she motioned to a stack of envelopes on my bed.

"I hope there's enough money left in your paycheck. I need to pay those bills."

Shame burst my bubble like a stiletto heel. I slapped my forehead. All of this cash juggling was proving to be a major hassle. Common sense urged me to ask Parker for help to put my financial situation in order, but the thought died before reaching my mouth. I just needed this one date to be spectacular. I'd work out the costs later.

The next day at lunch I barreled into my bank's local branch determined to do what I promised myself not to do: obtain a major credit card. Much more confident with the process, I sought out an account manager. A lovely woman helped me.

I said, *"I need a credit card."*

She typed my account information into the computer.

"Well, Miss Davis, with your account, if you want a credit card, we have one with zero percent interest for the first year, no annual fee, and you can earn mileage.

TIP: Before you get a credit card, check out the applications on the Internet, it's worth your time to be clear on the small print. Most credit card companies reserve the right to change the interest rate at any time, and change the contract if your payment doesn't arrive in time. Pay off the balance each month if you can … credit card debt is not a smart way to utilize your money and will drain your liquidity fast!

Okay, it only had zero percent interest for the first twelve billing cycles (one year), and then, Holy Smokes! Did it say they would charge 21.24% on purchases depending on my credit rating?! With Grandpa Wallace's advice ringing in my head "don't go into debt," I knew this was a major mistake. But, what else could I do? I promised myself to stick with my ATM debit card as much as possible and avoid going into debt.

I would only use the credit card for emergencies. I had a full year of no interest—so I have to keep up with my purchases. But, did I want to incur 21.24% on outstanding purchases? Heavens, no! I'd pay the balance each month and then get rid of the card after the first year. Period. I prided myself that I thought to ask, "Do you have a credit card that charges less interest after the first twelve months?"

She shook her head. *"With your credit rating and deposit amount, I'm afraid not."*

"What is my credit rating?"

"Looks like 723."

"How is that determined and can I check my report to see if it's accurate?"

"Sure." She nodded, and took a brochure out of her drawer. *"The Fair Credit Reporting Act requires the three consumer credit reporting agencies, Experian, Equifax and TransUnion to provide you with a free credit report, at your request, every 12 months. There's a central website www.annualcreditreport.com or you can call (877) 322-8228 and go from there. If you want more information just go to http://www.ftc.gov/bcp/conline/pubs/credit/freereports.shtm and the website outlines all the 'facts for consumers'. No need to spend your hard earned dollars for a credit report - this information is free! And, FICO scores come from this information.*

I said, "Thanks so much for the help. And, I will take the Visa."

Ah, the price of freedom. The ultimate test of self-discipline.

I was not yet a finance addict.

I was screwed.

4

I never should have spent money I didn't possess on that clingy, powder blue Stella McCartney dress and matching Jimmy Choo shoes. Without question, my outfit floored Alan. Within an hour, however, my ignorance of finance killed the love light.

The fact that I was late again should have been enough warning. I wouldn't have kept Alan waiting in the lobby if I could only remember what I did with my wallet.

I had this nagging sense I'd lost it.

I quickly turned the TV to CNBC as the newscaster declared the market closed down 175 points. I chanted, "Down one hundred and seventy five points," as I hustled around the apartment looking for my wallet. I snapped off the TV, stuffed a lipstick into my purse and bolted for the elevator. I'd worry about my wallet later.

Alan hustled me out to a waiting taxi. His eyes took in my dress, but his comment echoed his surprise that after four months of dating, he couldn't get used to me being late.

He did, however, stop in his tracks; hand on the taxi door, when I told him I thought I lost my wallet. He got all sorts of rigid when I admitted I hadn't reported it. Well, hell's bells. I was hurrying to be on time for our date!

I slid into the seat, thinking this evening wasn't starting well. At least the taxi was clean. Alan gave the taxi directions up-town, a frown marring his angelic face. I asked him if he had a bad day.

He rolled his eyes. "Terrible day. Never had one like it."

I said, "What do you mean?"

He gave me this look as if to say, dare I try? I should have known then that I'd already made his she's-not-going-to-make-it list.

I forged on. "Come on. Tell me. I'm a good listener."

Guess that convinced him, because he took a breath and launched.

"The Fed tightened unexpectedly this morning. The trading floor exploded and it wasn't even an FOMC meeting. I don't know if they've ever done that before! We were stunned. To make matters worse our Strategist was on an airplane. 120 phone lines lit at the same time. Everyone wanted out and we only had seconds! The noise was deafening. All I heard was SELL! SELL! SELL! Get out of everything ... NOW! The computer trading programs were moving at the speed of light!"

I wanted to rattle my head and say, *"The Fed did whaaaaat??? Sell what? Who's an FOMC?"* But, I squeezed his arm and said, "That's terrible. Are you all right?"

He ran a hand through his hair. "You should have seen it. The off the run five year note cratered in less than four and a half minutes. I've never witnessed anything like it." He shrugged, holding his palms open as if begging. *"We live and die off the government economic numbers and what the Fed does. Thank God I managed to sell just under a billion dollars worth of notes before 25 basis points up."*

My mind swirled. I wanted to say, "You lost me at cratered," but with CNBC urging me on, I managed to reply, *"Dare I ask you what a basis point is?"*

Favoring me with a frustrated look, he took the liberty to exhale a cleansing breath. *"Okay, Sam. A basis point is a term typically used to denote values under 1 percent. So, when the Fed raises interest rates by 25 basis points, that means one quarter of one percent (0.25%). 100 basis points is 1.00%. Get it?"*

Now, I was in deep. I nodded my head like one of those little plastic dolls in the back window of a passing car, then asked *"Okay, then why are you using the term, Fed, when before you said FOMC?"*

Slowly, he said, *"The Fed is short for Federal Reserve and connotes the 12 bank system that makes up the Federal Reserve. Each of the 12 regions has a governor and they have a seven member committee called the Federal Open Market Committee, which is responsible for raising and lowering interest rates through the discount rate and the overnight rate. Hence, FOMC. In addition, Sam, the President of the United States appoints the Federal Reserve Chairman. Alan Greenspan and Ben Bernanke have chaired this committee. Have you heard of them?"*

I said, "Hey, I thought Alan Greenspan still chaired the Federal Reserve."

He managed to grin. "He retired. I really need a martini."

Even though he left me in the dust, finance-wise, I kissed his cheek and whispered. "Anyone who survived the stock market today deserves a double."

Alan cringed. "The stock market?"

His arm stiffened under my hand as he stared at me in disbelief. "Forget what I said. I just wish I knew you were going to be late. I wouldn't have busted my tail to get here on time."

At our table, I felt his eyes on me while I read the menu, and thought, this is good. This is very good. I met his gaze, and grinned, letting him know his look reflected all the right thoughts. Now, I needed to hear them.

He came through in flying colors.

"Your eyes. That dress. You look so sexy. I can't concentrate on the menu."

I raised my martini to toast his, and grinned. "Thank you."

He sipped his drink. "And the martini's perfect. All's right with the world again."

I sipped my martini, and said, "I'm trying to make you forget the market dropped 175 points today."

You'd think I slapped him. First, disbelief flooded his eyes. His face actually turned red as he let his menu fall on his plate. He pressed fingers to his forehead as if in pain and whispered, "Oh, God, I don't need another bimbo."

To that same God, I silently cried, did he just say bimbo?

Stunned, I said, "What did you call me?"

He winced, squeezing his eyes shut before opening them to meet mine. Clearly, he hadn't expected me to hear.

"Sam, if I told you once, I've told you a hundred times. I work the bond market not the stock market. Didn't you listen to a word I said in the cab?"

The sadness in his voice rattled me. Somehow, I sensed more going on in his head than my misunderstanding his job.

"I heard you," I said, shrugging an almost bare shoulder. "I try to understand, Alan. It all sounds the same to me."

At that exact moment, the love light extinguished in his eyes and my heart stopped beating with his first sentence.

"Honey, listen to me. *The stock market and bond market are two different things. I trade the five year note. I work on a bond trading floor, in U.S. Government Securities. Not the stock trading floor.*"

At a complete loss with his explanation, I said, "Okay." I forced myself not to gulp my martini.

Now, as an aside, it took a few years after I totally screwed up my relationship with Alan, to finally take pains to appreciate everything he had said this fateful night. He worked in the bond market, not the stock market. To understand what happened on that hellish day on the trading floor, see APPENDIX B. Besides, when you earn thousands of dollars to invest you will want to know what your financial advisor says when she (or he) wants to explain a bad day—or a good one! And, super-important: If you hold any interest in becoming involved in real estate, and you should own your own place, this appendix details how interest rates move in the United States. This directly affects mortgage rates! Read APPENDIX B. Your future is at stake.

Meanwhile, Alan reached for my hand. I was about to get the great kiss-off.

"Samantha, I love your style. I love your beautiful baby blues, your hair, your sweet little nose. I love how it wrinkles up when you laugh, the way your mouth pouts before I kiss you. I love your jokes. But, playthings are a dime a dozen. I need a woman who thinks. One who cares about my career. Maybe, you're still a bit too young."

Too young? Plaything? My blood ran cold. I had to put my drink down, or toss it in his face. Outrage filled my head. I opened my mouth to speak and realized he was right. I deflated like a flat tire. We hadn't even ordered dinner and the night had unraveled. My inability to understand his business world ruined us as a couple.

Worse still, I spent half the month's paycheck on this damn outfit.

My mortification grew from the lethal mix of his insults, his sudden disappointment with me, and the fact that he spoke the truth. Needless to say, dinner bombed. Had Stella McCartney and Jimmy Choo arrived, they would have stripped me naked and left a note saying, 'Do Not Resuscitate.'

And, rightly so. Flirting with Alan wasn't enough. Flirting with finance wasn't enough. Alan lived and breathed finance for his living. He needed the love of his life to crave the same, and understand his world. Finance had yet to drug my system as it had his.

Alan dropped me off immediately after dinner. He didn't even kiss me good night.

I stood on the sidewalk, tears blurring my vision as his taxi melted away into the stream of tail lights. My heart ached as if kicked. In every other way, Alan and I made a perfect match. He dumped me because I couldn't tell a stock from a bond. I stood there still foolish enough to wonder why knowing the difference mattered.

5

I couldn't face my apartment. I walked down Third Avenue in a daze. I was glad for the dark. I was glad for the anonymity of New York streets because tears streamed down my cheeks, staining my dress. No one noticed. The regret in Alan's eyes haunted me as I walked. My bruised heart echoed my throbbing feet with every step I took.

At 65th Street, my gaze fell on Aunt Sally's apartment building. Aunt Sally, third cousin on my father's side, was ten years older than my mother. That's why she insisted I call her "Aunt." Family gossip had long died, but the story was that in her thirties, Sally dated a multi-millionaire and carried on with the man for sixteen years before he dumped her for a younger woman.

Aunt Sally walked away from the relationship with a quarter of a million dollars, but blew the entire amount on clothes and vacations. (The clothes thing must be genetic.) She believed that once she got over the hurt, she'd find another man.

But, the worst thing happened. Driving home from a party in Aspen, her car spun out on black ice. Aunt Sally shattered the windshield with her face, destroying not only her looks, but her future. Bell's Palsey paralyzed part of her face. Her friends couldn't handle her handicap, so invitations to parties dried up. As a "kept" woman for all those years, Sally never considered investing her money or starting a retirement account, not to mention she never had a career. Eventually, she managed to land a receptionist job with an investment bank, but the damage had been done.

Life as she knew it had been ruined at forty-eight years old.

Now, at 63, her looks long gone, the most she'd been able to do for herself was secure a rent-controlled, third story walk-up. As retirement approached, she'd made plans to move to a one bedroom apartment in a retirement village in West Palm Beach, Florida.

The Florida sun would be good for her.

I wiped my eyes, spotting her apartment buzzer. We'd shared dinner last month. She knew about Alan. I pressed the button, thinking that Aunt Sally was my saving grace at this very sick-in-the-pit-of-my-belly moment.

I choked back a fresh sob. "Aunt Sally? It's Samantha. Can I come up?"

"Sam! Sure, honey."

The door buzzed. As penance, I climbed the three flights teetering on my four-inch Choos. They were the first things Aunt Sally noticed.

"Nice shoes! Did Alan buy them for you?"

My heart leapt into my throat. I swallowed to keep the razor out of my retort. "I spent half a month's paycheck buying this outfit and got dumped for it!"

Only the left side of Aunt Sally's face showed surprise. The right side just sat there. If she didn't notice, I certainly did.

She peered closer. "Alan dumped you? Oh! You've been crying," she observed with half a mouth.

I waved a weary hand suddenly wondering why I came here.

"He thinks I'm a bubble brain because I don't know stocks from bonds or T-bills from tampons." I rolled my eyes at my own stupid joke.

Sally was already pouring me a glass of cheap wine. Jay Leno was talking to both of us through the TV, his words practically inaudible, as the studio audience laughed at his jokes. "Well, that's just dumb of Alan. I don't know about financial stuff, either. A lot of women don't." She winked at me with the good side of her face.

She handed me a glass of cheap white wine. I followed her the entire two feet from her kitchen counter to her vintage, leather sofa. Her apartment wasn't much bigger than my studio. That wouldn't be so bad if there wasn't clutter everywhere. I could see her unmade bed through the bedroom door, fashion magazines and romance novels making a small mountain atop the night stand, a pile of clothes blocking the closet door.

I took one sip of the bad wine. My stomach clenched as realization dawned: If I didn't get my act together, this would be me in thirty-five years. Lonely and poor, wearing vintage couture, living in a thimble-sized space smelling of this morning's bacon, drinking shitty wine and watching TV on a Thursday night. Was this all that remained after riding the high life on someone else's shoulders?

Silently thanking whatever angel steered me to 65th Street, I'd seen enough. "You know? My bad date made me more tired than I thought. I have to go."

Aunt Sally twisted around on the sofa so her good side would face me. "Don't you worry about Alan, honey. Another wonderful man will come along and you won't have to worry your pretty little head about a thing."

I kissed her and left before I threw up my wine.

The next morning, I got up early, careful not to wake Parker who worked nights at the restaurant. I dressed and left for work. I couldn't even buy a cup of coffee because my wallet was still missing.

I needed to get a grip … immediately.

Not surprising, my colleague, Morgan Price, had been at her desk for an hour already. She was only two years older than me, but had already earned her law degree. As a peer, she was, without a doubt, the smartest woman I ever met. Morgan was down-to-earth, taking charge of her life and career with the easy grace of a dancer.

Everyone needed a mentor. I had secretly dubbed her as mine. This morning, it felt as though the sun began to shine when she stopped at my desk.

"You don't look so good," she said and checked her watch. "And, in early. Uh-oh. What's wrong?"

I felt suspiciously calm as I told her I blew it with Alan because I didn't understand his job at Credit Suisse.

Morgan's gaze grew cautious. "Do you care to understand, Sam?"

I couldn't believe she'd nailed the truth. I said, "Up until last night, no. I didn't care. It's all mumbo-jumbo to me."

Morgan jumped all over that one. She slotted me for dinner that night. With a good meal under our belts, I was going to begin my official finance training.

I watched her walk away, all chic, dark-haired sexy and professional, and realized that somewhere between graduating early from high school, finishing law school and passing the bar by the age of twenty three, Morgan had discovered the secret to financial and personal independence: Confidence.

Shoot. Confidence was my middle name. I was loaded with it. Well, at least I knew how to dress! But, now I discovered a new target for confidence: Finance.

Later that morning, I spotted an e-mail from Alan. Despite my new epiphany on confidence, butterflies ka-boomed inside my stomach, knocking into each other so badly, I had to press a hand to my middle.

My mouse couldn't move quickly enough to open the e-mail. The message read:

Good morning, Samantha,

If you haven't found your wallet yet, this is what you should do to prevent identify theft:

FIRST- Call the fraud departments of the three major credit bureaus. Request a "fraud alert" be placed on your file.

SECOND—Contact your credit card companies, utilities, banks and other lenders and speak to someone in the security or fraud department. Follow up your phone call with a letter. Close all accounts that have been tampered with. When opening any new accounts choose your PIN numbers carefully. Don't use your mother's maiden name, your birth date, the last four digits of your Social Security number, or your phone number.

THIRD—File a report with the police in the community where the identify theft took place. Get a copy of the police report.

If you think you might be the victim of identity theft or if your wallet or purse is lost or stolen … NOTIFY THESE AGENCIES RIGHT AWAY:

YOUR LOCAL POLICE DEPARTMENT

MAJOR CREDIT CARD COMPANIES
American Express	*800-441-0519*
Visa	*800 VISA911*
MasterCard	*800-307-7309*
Discover	*800-347-2683*
Diners Club	*800-234-6377*
Carte Blanche	*800-234-6377*

CREDIT REPORT BUREAUS
Equifax	*800-525-6285*
Experian	*800-397-3742*
TransUnion	*800-680-7289*
SOCIAL SECURITY ADMINISTRATION	*800-772-1213*

YOUR STATE'S DRIVER'S LICENSE OFFICE

FEDERAL TRADE COMMISSION (FTC) IDENTITY THEFT www.ftc.gov
HOTLINE - 877-IDTHEFT

YOUR LOCAL BANK BRANCH

ATM CARD

I hope this helps with the lost wallet. It's really important that you protect yourself from someone stealing your identity. Got to get back to trading … BONDS, remember?

Cordially, Alan

Cordially? There was no love in the word, cordially. Zero. Zip. None. His e-mail was motivated solely from his financial obligation toward the monetary jungle of my life. At least he cared enough to send me some advice to avoid financial harm from losing my wallet.

But, I'd lost him for sure.

The knowledge left a dent in my ticker. I rubbed my chest to ease the pain.

In the meantime, I had to protect my identity. I printed out his e-mail and began the phone calls right away. It proved to be the most exhausting hour in my life. I learned that with today's savvy technology thieves, losing my wallet could literally rob me of my identity and screw up my credit for years.

6

A chardonnay in hand at seven o'clock, I amused myself watching the other patrons until Morgan joined me for dinner. She ordered a twin glass then met my gaze like a true mentor.

She said, "Now, tell me what happened with Alan last night. Don't mince words."

I recounted our conversation verbatim. It really irked me that he thought I was dumb. I'm smart, damn him. I just wasn't interested enough to sit down and learn the details.

Morgan sipped her wine and said, "I can see his point, you know."

I gave her my perfected, you've-got-to-be-kidding stare and said, "Are you a traitor to woman-kind?"

She laughed. "No, Sam! Today's women can't afford to be ignorant about finance."

I felt a twinge inside my head telling me I was about to accept the attitude change I felt prodding me at Aunt Sally's. I braced myself, knowing the muscle I'd have to flex now was my brain. I sat back in my chair, cupping my wine in my hand.

"Okay, I'll listen."

She leaned in, tapping her perfectly manicured fingernail on the table to emphasize her point.

"Understanding finances is like learning a foreign language. Once you grasp the basic grammar, the rest falls into place."

Her words washed over my thoughts like some new exotic drug. I laughed and told her that I flunked French, was probably helpless, but I loved the allure of a foreign language.

She wouldn't react to my joke. She was dead serious.

I shook my head. Despite my desire to change, the finance side of my brain felt like life had dealt it one too many Margaritas. It felt numb, impenetrable.

Morgan just smiled at me. She said, "Maybe you just need to hear a woman explain stocks and bonds."

That made sense. Women and men did speak different languages. Didn't someone write something about Mars men and Venus babes? So, I listened:

"Well, usually the term, "the market" refers to the stock market, and more specifically to the 30 stocks in the Dow Jones Industrial Average (DJIA), which has nothing to do with Bonds," Morgan said, biting a cashew.

My enthusiasm melted. I didn't understand a word she said.

She pushed her sleeves up. *"Okay, let's say that finance is like a foreign language, like French or Spanish. Once you learn what the terms mean, understanding it becomes simple. The best part is that learning financial terms is much easier than learning a foreign language."*

I sipped my wine and leaned in for more. This track, I could follow.

"Let's look at 'bonds' first because that's what Alan does. The best way to explain a bond is that it's basically a loan. You loan your money to someone like a bank or the US government by buying bonds. The institution to which you lend your money then pays you to borrow your money. The terms used in this context are bills, notes, and bonds, but 'bonds' is a generic term used to explain the entire market. The money paid out is called interest, and the amount of interest paid is determined by how safe the investment is. When Alan says he works in bonds, that means he deals with debt issued by a government or corporation guaranteeing payment of the original investment plus interest by a specified future date."

It almost registered. I asked her to repeat the information again. Just to be sure.

She smiled, undaunted, God love her.

"To put it in simpler terms, it's like your parents' mortgage payment. They buy a house, borrow money and pay back the purchase price plus a certain amount of interest. Let's say you have $100,000 and you can loan it to me or the waiter—she smiled at the waiter as he delivered our meals—*for a new home. You have a pretty good idea I'll pay you back, because I have a steady job. The waiter, however, has no idea how much he'll make tonight or even if the restaurant will be in business tomorrow night.* Thank goodness he'd stepped away. Wouldn't want to ruin his night. *For me, you'll charge 2.5% interest and for the waiter, you'll charge 8%. More for the waiter because he's a bigger risk that you'll get paid back. So, with this thought, rating agencies were created to rank all bonds. Standard & Poor's and Moody's are the largest agencies. In my example, a rating agency would make me a AAA (triple A) rate and the waiter a D rate. This is basically the way the bond market works."*

I practically choked on my own excitement. "I get that!"

Morgan laughed. "See? It's simple once you understand the language."

She sipped her wine. Pointing at me she said, *"Now, back to the differences between stocks and bonds."*

"A stock is part ownership in a corporation. When you buy stock, you actually purchase part of a corporation. So, if the company does well, the price of your stock goes up. If it does poorly, the price goes down. The term 'stock' can be interchanged with 'equity' and 'shares'. So, when you purchase a part of a company, you buy 'stock' in it. So, what Alan does is completely different from the stock market."

I repeated, *"A bond is like a loan, and a stock is like buying part of a corporation (or ownership)."*

Morgan nodded. *"Yes. The 'market' refers to only 30 of the top corporations which are listed on the Dow Jones Industrial Average (DJIA) and represent the general feel of all the stocks traded in the U.S."*

I slapped my forehead. The 'market' really didn't have anything to do with bonds. Now, I understood.

Morgan clapped her hands. "Bravo, my friend!"

Finally, it all seemed so simple. I wished I could rewind the past twenty four hours to replay my date with Alan. Was I kidding? I inwardly smacked myself. Alan had called me a bimbo and meant it. Understanding this finance stuff gave me a heady feeling. I liked it much better than needing to prove myself to Alan.

I grinned at Morgan. Not even the amazing Alan was as clear explaining finance as Morgan had been. She was absolutely right. <u>Finance is just a different language</u>. All I had to was <u>learn the details.</u>

I bit a morsel of food from my fork. My mind had been altered. The information clicked. I had taken the next step in securing my finance addiction. It felt good.

I wanted more!

7

My financial euphoria abruptly came to a halt as I stared at my credit card bill for $1269 at the end of the month. I wanted to scream. The Stella McCartney dress and Jimmy Choo shoes sat in my closet as monuments to my stupidity and poor financial planning. I was broke. A knot as big as the dress itself lodged in my throat as I promised myself to pay off the charge in three months.

Sure. And Publisher's Clearing House would knock on the door with one of those oversized, bazillion-dollar checks any second now.

It was a no-brainer. I could achieve financial knowledge and independence. I felt sure about everything else. Why not finance?

I needed to feel finance in my blood.

I needed to change my focus.

I started reading the business section of the New York Times. I let CNBC run while eating dinner alone, trying to get a feel for the jargon. Every day I snagged a Wall Street Journal at the office. Morgan told me if I read the two columns on the front page, left for the business news, and right for the world news, I would have a synopsis of all the important news.

My job became the love of my life. I ratcheted up my already-implemented approach to success, and every legal resource group on every floor soon knew my name. The big offices took notice. My superiors began assigning really interesting cases to me.

I was making a name for myself.

One month later, the Personnel Department phoned me. *I was now eligible for the 401(k) retirement plan, and should attend a seminar outlining my benefits and choices.* I was booked for two hours on Friday.

I could do this. Like the sci-fi Borg Empire from Star Trek, I was assimilating finance.

But, on Friday, a momentary panic set in. Would I understand the jargon? How would I know which choices were good? I dropped by Morgan's office minutes before the seminar.

She laughed at my concern and said, "Just listen and you'll understand."

Two hours' worth of material? I wanted to make the right retirement decisions. Shades of Aunt Sally haunted me.

"Sam, this is just a retirement plan to set up now, while you're young. *The advice I've gotten from many Financial Planners is to max-out your contribution.*"

I leaned forward and said, *"Explain what you mean by maxing out my contribution."*

She said, *"Okay. Your goal should be to contribute as much as you comfortably can to your 401 (k) because the company will offer an excellent matching plan to the amount you contribute. Sam, think FREE MONEY from the company. Also, 401(k) plans take advantage of government tax laws for deferring your money. The company is having the seminar to outline the benefits of a 401(k) and the investment options. Note to reader: Just be careful of any plans investing in 100% of your company stock. Don't forget WorldCom and Enron went bankrupt and employees with their retirement dollars exclusively in the company stock lost everything.*"

I thought my eyes would roll back in my head. I didn't understand any of this. I needed it explained in a language I could understand.

She lifted a knowing finger. *"Think of it as the make-up you use on your face every day. The 401(k) or retirement plan is like foundation. It is the base of everything else you put on. Think of the investments in your 401(k) as mascara, lip stick, and eye shadow. With the foundation as the base, the rest is used to complete the look. Your Retirement plan (in our case a 401(k)) is the base, and your investments will complete the plan."*

I nodded slowly. Morgan always had a great way of easily explaining the complicated.

"Good. *Now, figure you'll basically have one foundation that works for you—it's the right color, shade and texture. That foundation or retirement plan (could be a 401(k), 403(b), IRA Roth, Traditional IRA, Rollover, etc.) is the corner-stone to the investments for your retirement fund's growth. Everything else—or the makeup you choose—is built upon this base. Once the foundation is laid, we add the products that work for us."*

I snapped my fingers. I got it! *She was saying make-up options are wide ranging and vary dramatically, just like investment options which are wide ranging and vary dramatically. Just like I choose blush, lip stick, lip liner, mascara, eye shadow, and/or eyeliner, I can choose different investments.*

Morgan clapped. "Now you're ready."

I sank back into the chair. The thought occurred to me, so I asked, *"What kinds of investments are we talking about?"*

Morgan lifted a tailored shoulder as if everyone knew this. *"You can choose investments for your retirement account such as: large cap, small cap, international, aggressive growth, income, high yield."*

A dazed look crossed my face. I could feel it. Her eyes danced with merriment. She was having too damn much fun at my expense. I couldn't help but laugh at my own insecurity.

She said, "Don't worry. They'll teach you all about these investments in the two hour meeting. *Just remember when they discuss an investment, approach it like a new type of mascara which you haven't tried before. A stock is a stock and a bond is a bond; and mascara is mascara, you just need to figure out the different spin on each particular product."*

"Look, Sam", she said taking out a piece of paper, *"There are only four things you can do with your money. One, keep it in cash like a money market or Certificate of Deposit (CD). Two, buy ownership in a company which is a stock and also called equity. Three, loan your money which is a bill, note or bond. And four, buy commodities like gold, orange juice, oil, etc. Every investment is one of these four: cash, equity, bond or commodity—everything else is a spin on one of these particular four choices. I'll tell you about the spin later, but I'm sure you've heard the term 'derivative', which just means derived from something.* Now, go—you're late for the meeting."

8

I ran out of her office feeling much better. I was primed for the retirement lingo. But, two hours of investment decisions meant my choices would be critical to my retirement, which seemed so far off. But, financial independence in my golden years hung in the balance (even if it just ends up being a saving account for a face-lift). I was entering an arena of which I knew zip and hoped not to get zapped. So, to be sure I got the info straight, I took a front row seat.

Yes, I was prepared to brown-nose to the hilt.

Penny Pincher greeted us all, again. Of course, inspecting her gorgeous black wool suit, led to her accessories of pearls and ... hello? What's this? Penny sported a diamond engagement ring the size of a meteor. Well, good for her.

Ms. Pincher began:

"Since you've been here two months, all of you are eligible for the company's 401(k) which is also called a company-sponsored retirement plan. This 401(k) plan is defined as a plan which allows you to save money for retirement in a tax deferred manner.* You can choose to deduct part of your paycheck, which reduces taxable income and place it into an investment portfolio. Employers may choose to match a portion of the employee's contribution up to 50 percent. These investments grow tax free until the money is withdrawn during retirement.

This must be the free money part Morgan was talking about. I put money into my retirement plan, and the company adds the same amount as an incentive for saving. Incentives like that, I like!

*Note: A 401(k) plan is offered by private corporations and 403(b) plan is offered to employees of non-profit organizations. There are also other names of retirement plans and which one you choose (or are offered) will depend on what type of company you work for.

Penny continued. *"The 401(k) plan we offer at this company has many investment options to choose from and they are outlined in the brochure we just gave you."* Looking no less than an executive Vanna White, she pointed to a chart on a stand. *"Please look at this chart of different mutual and index funds offered."* (Remember that the Year to Date (YTD) numbers and ratings change frequently, so it is important to double check the information before making a decision).

I looked down at the various funds - where do I begin? The list was two pages long and the categories included: Mid-Cap Growth, World Stock, Specialty—Precious Metals and Health and Financial, Muni National Intermediate, High Yield Muni, Large-Cap, Small Cap, Mid Cap, Aggressive Growth. I felt like Lara Croft on an expedition in an ancient cave. And, then there were different Fund companies: American, AIM, Fidelity, BlackRock and Morgan Stanley just to name a few. Where's a girl to start?

There are great comparative tools on the Internet and all major investment houses have different websites to guide you through this decision. A few include:

https://www.tdameritrade.com/trade/mutualfunds.html
http://personal.fidelity.com/planning/retirement/investment_overview.shtml

Pointing at the brochure, Penny Pincher went on, *"This page is just the first of the funds offered from which you'll choose, but to make it easier we break them down into different strategies based on age."*

Jeeze, so many funds! What in the heck do they all mean?

One of the attendees asked, *"Does my age matter when I choose an investment?"*

She nodded. *"Yes, I'll explain more in a minute. What we do is take a percentage from your paycheck before taxes and invest it in the mutual funds and index funds that you choose from this form. Please keep in mind while reviewing these funds that past performance is no guarantee of future results."*

"The percentage taken bi-weekly from your paycheck also allows you to take advantage of the concept of 'dollar cost averaging'. Because we are buying the fund shares bi-monthly and the price is fluctuating; the amount of money we use will sometimes buy more shares and sometimes buy less. For example, if the fund shares are $10 this month and we are contributing $100, then we buy 10 shares. However, if the shares go down to $8 next month we can buy 12.5 shares; if price is $12 per share, we can buy 8.3 shares and so on".

Penny glanced around the room. "Any questions so far?"

I smiled and shook my head. This information was sinking in. I just put her words into Morgan's suggestion of turning the finance options into make-up. The 401(k) was my foundation, and the chart above offered all the wonderful mascaras, blushes and lipsticks from which I could choose. Not bad.

A silly little thrill ran through me. The flush of financial understanding satisfies almost as much as chocolate. Hey, I said almost!

Penny seemed satisfied with our expressions, too, because she launched away ...

"Your investment options in a 401(k) will primarily be made up of Mutual Funds and Index Funds. The Mutual Funds will comprise some combination of stocks, bonds, commodities (oil, gold, silver, etc.) and cash. Mutual funds offer professional management, a low entry rate and diversification.

Now, Index funds track the various indices which is a generic name used for the Dow Jones Industrial Average (DJIA), Standard and Poors 500 (S&P 500), Russell 2000, etc. Index Funds do not have professional management, and therefore, often have lower fees to manage them."

A redhead in a copper sweater and navy skirt raised her hand. *"If Index Funds don't have professional management, then who manages them?"*

Red echoed my thoughts.

"Index funds purchase a certain index, like the S&P 500 and have weighted positions in the various companies in the index. It is a set strategy and is considered 'buy and hold'. Therefore, they are not actively managed and have lower management fees."

Penny continued. *"Next, let's address the age factor. Each 'fund' has an objective which includes risk tolerance and return."*

Hmm. That had me thinking. *Risk tolerance meant how risky a fund would be. Return would signify how much my investment would yield.*

"These objectives are primarily divided by, and suggested, based on the age of the investor. The theory being the longer you can stay in the fund, the better your chances to make a steady return. The younger you are, the more aggressive you can be, the older, the less aggressive.

She did another Vanna White towards a chart perched on the white-board. *"The brochure outlines the following strategies based on age, and this list is a nice framework to choose your retirement investments:*

__Aggressive Growth__ (Ages 20—30 years old) - a 100% stock portfolio which invests in small capitalization (Small Cap) companies that are aggressively entering the marketplace. The newest, latest greatest technology is the cornerstone for these types of funds. It invests in both international and domestic stocks.

__Growth__ (Ages 30—40) Invests in some small companies, but seeks to provide long-term capital growth through a diversified mix of domestic and international equity (stock) funds.

__Growth & Dividend__ (Ages 40—50) Provides long-term capital growth and income by investing in a highly diversified and balanced mix of both equity and fixed income funds. But, primarily invests in established companies that pay a dividend.

__Dividend Growth__ (Ages 50—60) invests only in large capitalization (Large Cap) companies that pay a significant dividend, with almost half in fixed income funds.

Conservative Growth (Ages 60 years old ++) Seeks to provide long-term capital preservation, with some total return and growth potential, by investing in a diversified mix of fixed-income funds with a smaller portion in equity funds.

She grinned again, leaning forward as if we were co-conspirators.

"Anyone in the room over thirty?"

Heck, everyone in the room looked under thirty. And, I like the idea of being aggressive which would translate into more money. Cool!

Penny said, *"Once you get more money, you might want to even ignore the age limits and mix them up a bit to suit your personal risk tolerance level. We'll come back to 'aggressive growth' in a minute."*

Then, she looked very serious!

"There is always risk involved in investing, and the risk is that your investment could decrease in value. The general rule is the higher the return, the greater the risk; the lower the return, the lower the risk. So, a small company with new technology is a greater risk, but offers better potential return than, say a US Government Security which has a relatively low rate of return but almost no risk."

"If the investment sounds too good to be true—IT IS! If we check a particular sector fund, say energy, and the average return is 3%, and then a manager claims to make 9%, we know something is wrong. Having said that, our company does due diligence (in other words, thoroughly checks out every manager) on all the funds we hire for our retirement plans.

For further discussion of this, please search "risk reward chart" on the web.

I wondered if Alan would jump at the opportunity to test risk, since he's a bond trader and they have the least risk of all. I felt a tad superior just considering higher risk stocks.

I glanced at the packet Penny's assistant had passed around. There were hundreds of funds to choose from. My head started to swim, but I realized each fund could be a potential opportunity for more cash. I raised my hand.

"There are a gazillion funds listed here. How do I choose the right ones for me?"

She beamed. "That's an excellent question. *Which do you choose? Always look for a fund with a long term return of five years or more. As I said before, our company does due diligence on each fund manager, which means we investigate the investment company to confirm all material facts, before allowing them to be part of your 401(k) plan. It is very important to you that we are making sure your money is in good hands."*

I liked that! Nice to know the company has my back. I glanced back at the list of fund managers and their return rates. I realized some were higher than others. It just zings your nervous system with delight when you realize a new financial fact. I raised my hand again.

"Does picking a long term track record and/or the highest return for the previous year make a difference?"

Her exuberance at my question felt almost as good as my question!

"Yes!" She said. *"You've got the idea now. But, different strategies will* do *better in given years. There is a great chart which lists how different asset classes did in different years. Click on this link to access the chart:*

http://www.callan.com/research/download/?file=periodic%2ffree%2f548.pdf

As you can see over the years the sector that does the best varies appreciably."

Next to me another hand went up. This guy looked preppy. Sort of Clark Kent-ish. He asked, *"What are the advantages of choosing Mutual Funds over Index Funds?"*

Penny replied, *"When you choose a mutual fund, your money is professionally managed. The cost to buy in is low, and the professionals holding the mutual fund will diversify the money, meaning you own* many stocks and bonds for a small entry cost. Index funds do not need expensive professional management or research analysts. They parallel an "index" which as I mentioned earlier is like the DJIA, S&P500, NASDAQ 100, Russell 2000, etc. The most common index fund tracks the S&P 500 by purchasing all 500 stocks using the same percentages as the index."

He continued. "So, how do you know which fund, or group of funds, to choose and which funds to stay away from?"

"You really should check the history behind a mutual fund before committing your hard earned dollars to it. "Now, this is important, so listen up! Some funds that do poorly will change their name and have the look and feel of a new fund. It's a technique used to manipulate the return numbers. I'd steer clear of those."

"Let's take a quick break and we'll meet back here in 15 minutes."

The redhead was in the ladies room when I arrived and had killer new shoes on! Multi-colored Prada. I'd die for them! Have to go shopping this weekend for sure! Well, shopping for great bargains anyway!

9

Penny glanced around the room. "Once again, is anyone here over thirty?" She asked more directly this time.

We surreptitiously glanced at each other to see if anyone would admit such a fate. No one raised a hand. Penny rubbed her hands together with glee. She was actually enjoying herself. I found her enthusiasm contagious.

"This is wonderful. *Then, let's concentrate on Aggressive Growth because you're in your 20's!!! This means an all stock (equity) portfolio.*"

(No bonds—sorry, Alan!)

"*When I say, Aggressive, I mean new, small companies that have the potential to do BIG things. In the early 90's, Microsoft and Dell fell into this category; both were trading around $1.10—ooh! In the 2000's we could have jumped back into Apple and done pretty well for ourselves. If only we knew then what we know now!*"

So, I figured, if my 401(k) is the foundation, then Aggressive Growth must be the hottest latest new look in blush, mascara and lip stick! A small tingle began in the base of my spine. I could actually be financially set in my retirement.

I raised my hand. "Let me be sure I understand. You're saying that now is the best time to risk investing in new companies because

I'm young. I'll make so much money I can wear Christian Louboutin shoes for life!"

Penny laughed. *"Remember what happened when the dot-com bubble burst! The Aggressive Growth portfolios took a beating."*

"However, having said that," Penny continued, *"many companies fell by the wayside also. It's a very risky place for your money to be, but if you hold for ten years or longer, and have professional management chances are you'll do very well. That's the beauty of making this type of investment at a young age."*

Funny thing. I started to salivate at the thought of my mere 6% investment becoming a stockpile of cash in my retirement years. Why didn't Aunt Sally do this? I was determined not to make the same mistake. My heart pounded quietly beneath my blazer. My ears became antennae for the finance lingo. My head buzzed with understanding. I leaned forward, poised for financial success. I wanted to know more!

"So, you may want to know exactly what Aggressive Growth is!"

She gave the guy next to me a dreamy look as she said, *"Aggressive Growth is a 100% stock or equity portfolio comprised of various mutual and index funds. These funds seek to provide long-term capital growth through both domestic and international funds. Sometimes, the strategies can be complex, but by having professional management you are 'hiring' the best to watch over your money."*

She continued. *"Mutual and Index Funds come in 'families.' These 'families' are just the names of the companies that manage them. For example, Fidelity, Wells Fargo, Advantage Funds, INVESCO, Nuveen, etc. Investment houses also have their own funds, Morgan Stanley, Wells Fargo, JP Morgan, etc. Your 401(k) Aggressive Growth portfolio might include a listing like this:*

Allianz Global Investors
Oppenheimer International Small Company Fund
INVESCO Russell 2000 Index
Fidelity Advisor Technology Fund
Don't forget to note the overseas specialty funds. You'll discover that these are usually a great area to make your money work!"

Clark Kent raised his hand again. *"How are the professional managers at these mutual funds and index funds paid?"*

Penny raised her eyebrows as if to say, hold on to your hats for this one. *"All businesses incur general costs. Mutual funds and index funds are no exception. However, since these are investment companies, the Securities and Exchange Commission (SEC) regulates and oversees the costs."*

"There are two types of fees: 'Shareholder Fees' which can include redemption fees; purchase fees; exchange fees; and 'Account Fees' and 'Annual Fund Operating Expenses' which include management fees; distribution (and/or service) 12b-1 fees; other expenses; and, total annual fund operating expenses.

"Index Funds can have expense ratios as low as 0.18% (or 18 basis points), while actively managed funds can have an expense ratios over 3.0% (or 300 basis points). Fees and expenses vary from fund to fund. An international mutual fund is more expensive to manage than an S&P 500 index fund for obvious reasons."

I could grasp that by obvious reasons she meant it costs more for Chanel mascara than for Cover Girl because Chanel comes from France and Cover Girl is domestic.

[Note to reader: To calculate the exact fees you pay for your mutual and index funds, the Securities and Exchange Commission has a cost calculator you can access at www.sec.gov/investor/tools. I would recommend using this cost calculator before giving your hard earned $$$ to anyone.]

By the time Penny finished, I felt like I had met a tornado head on, withstood its worst and returned safely to Kansas instead of Oz. I didn't feel mystified any longer. My body warmed with the rush of financial well-being. I was on the road to financial security. My age permitted me to choose an aggressive growth portfolio. I invested the suggested maximum of 6% for my future. I knew the 6% deduction from my paycheck would pinch my already tight income, but I'd work it out. I'd also have to work out my bills with Parker and pay off my credit card.

That reality quickly checked the warm-fuzzy feelings.

Only one solution loomed before me: No more shopping, and work, work, work.

I took one more look at my portfolio choices, held them to my nose smelling the prospects of money, then headed back to work.

Saturday morning found me at the office, lost in cyberspace. My boss entrusted me with a case tracking a rogue bond trader. The fact that he was a bond trader made me think of Alan. I felt a butterfly or two attempt to takeoff in my gut, but crash instead.

I missed Alan.

I battled loneliness daily.

Admitting the truth hurt. I consoled myself thinking that Alan would never stoop to the debauchery this rogue trader used to fleece his company and hide millions overseas. I should be glad to have known such a fine, upstanding man.

My little voice replied, Oh, cut the crap, Stella. He called you a bimbo then dumped you!

So, I changed tactics.

I dropped Alan from my thoughts like a basket of dirty laundry.

Instead, I imagined that searching small banks in Third World countries where this rogue might have hidden the money was the task of a superhero. I likened myself to Wonder Woman, or a Jedi knight searching the galaxy for Klingons. Oh, wait, I'm mixing up Star Wars with Star Trek, but you get my gist. Pursuing this case raised my self-esteem. I didn't need Alan! Besides, if I discovered the hidden money my esteem would sky rocket not only in my eyes, but in the eyes of my boss … and ultimately, be reflected in a fatter paycheck.

Now, that mattered.

By two o'clock, reality set in. This rogue bond trader was slick. I'd love to give him James Bond qualities, but in reality, he was a short, dumpy money genius with greasy hair and the mind of a felon. We had to nail this guy. But, not today. A headache brewed behind my eyes. It was time to go. I shut down my computer and headed for the door. The only way to cure a headache would be to visit Bloomingdale's for the afternoon.

Uh-oh. With my retirement deduction and debts to pay, I could only browse.

The thought evaporated when I ran into Morgan at the elevator.

"Surprised to see you here," she said, admiration lacing her voice.

I grinned and said, "It's the new me."

"Then we need to celebrate. How about we go downtown tonight? My friend can put us on the list at Barbachine."

Barbachine! The absolutely hottest spot in town. I wanted in.

Morgan said, "Great. Let's meet at my apartment at nine."

I headed for Bloomie's feeling ten feet tall. After all, if I hadn't been working on a Saturday, I never would have run into Morgan. Tonight we'd be dancing with all the beautiful people. The Jimmy Choos were coming out of the box!

Alas, my euphoria became my budget's downfall once I smelled the sweet perfume of new couture at Bloomingdale's. I managed to avoid the designer section, but lost control on the third floor.

When I saw them, I had to have the latest rage!

I tried on ten different styles. A hot black pair of Cynthia Rowley's pants fit perfectly. I choked when they rang up at one hundred and eighty dollars. But, no. I paid for them with my credit card, as the debit card couldn't handle a purchase this month.

Next, I found this sexy black top and realized my Jimmy Choos were powder blue. They wouldn't do tonight, after all. I headed off to the shoe department.

So, here I was, financially strung-out, and still willing to cruise the road I would one day call, Disaster Spending. Sadly for me, my finance addiction hadn't taken root. But did I acknowledge my new rules with credit cards or lack of discipline with a to-die-for opportunity to party at Barbachine tonight? Naaaaaaaah!

10

I woke at noon on Sunday. The inside of my eyelids felt gritty from too much partying. I laid there on my bed; eyes closed, with the alarm clocks electric, red numbers reflecting 12:08' against the back of my eyelids. Was all that money I spent on my new clothes worth the night at Barbachine?

My little voice answered. Of course not, Stella. You knew it wouldn't be. (I don't know why I call myself, Stella. Samantha is a perfectly good name.)

Truth was, my euphoria deflated moments after leaving Barbachine. I'd had fun, but I could have worn a dozen outfits I already owned. The knowledge that I had increased my debt because I fed some personal insecurity knocked the knees from under me—even if I was lying down.

I had to get a grip on my spending.

The muffled silence of the apartment surrounded my head like a Russian muff. Parker spent most days at the restaurant prepping for the night's cooking. This made great roommate arrangements in a small place, but I sure missed her. I missed her upbeat attitude. I missed her promises that life would be great for us in New York. She didn't seem to be struggling with her money like I was. I could use some of her insights right now.

To add to my misery, Parker was dating a new guy. Another chef. I was happy for her, really, but the emptiness of a significant other in my life nipped at my neck like a designer tag in a wool sweater.

Parker's absence exaggerated my solitude.

Therein lay my saddest problem.

Last night, I hadn't met anyone who held a candle to Alan. I avoided thinking about him, and couldn't help wondering if I spent money I didn't have to make myself feel better about losing him. Damn! A lose-lose situation. I'd have to re-think my thinking here!

I needed coffee.

I padded into the kitchen area.

I plugged in the coffee pot only to have my sight assaulted by the neatly stacked pile of bills on my side of the kitchen counter. A note perched on top of the bills.

Parker wrote: "I miss you. I'm off tomorrow night. Let's have dinner."

Elation was my first reaction.

My second was … Uh-oh.

I glanced around the tiny space. Every corner, nook and surface was littered with my stuff. The week's outfits. Dirty socks. Magazines. Hair brush and clips. A tin of Altoids. My black purse. A grey sweater. My grey purse. Shoes and sneakers tumbling over each other like drunks. My night stand was stacked with magazines and books, my keys, my emaciated new wallet since I never recovered my old one, leather gloves. My new pants, top and shoes sprawled on the floor. Any outfit that cost $412.49 in money I didn't possess didn't belong on the floor!

Slowly, I turned on my heel to glance at Parker's side of the room. Pristine. Her bed was made. Sheets and blankets folded in hospital corners, for goodness sake. A white down quilt lay at the foot of her bed. Not a stitch of clothing hung out of her dresser. The warm mahogany had been polished. A bottle of her favorite perfume, a small jewelry box and her silver brush and comb reflected in the dresser's surface.

Reality hit.

All the discipline I had focused on work seemed to have missed our apartment. My space, no larger than a hallway, screamed of a depressed personality. Shoot! I was dodging loneliness by working my tail off. I still hadn't achieved personal satisfaction for the sheer joy of accomplishment.

I mentally shook myself. No more!

I felt like King-Kong beating his chest.

I glanced at my bills again. Okay. I'd order some Chinese food for lunch then open those. Meanwhile, it was time to flex my muscles.

I would unleash Samantha's white tornado!

Two hours later, the apartment gleaming about me, my meal of chicken and cashew nuts lost its fattening attraction. My bills far exceed my means to pay them.

How did people survive in New York City?

I scribbled a note back to Parker. "Miss you, too! Would love to have dinner."

I was going to come clean with her, too.

The next night, Parker chatted happily at dinner. It was easy sliding into banter over her boyfriend, Franco, clothes, and the great time Morgan and I had at Barbachine's. Parker regaled me with tales of celebrities dining at the restaurant and how one of Martha Stewart's minions spilled red wine on her white wool dress and came charging into the kitchen, pulled her skirt over her butt to rinse the wine out and lo' and behold, the girl wore no panties.

One of the chefs almost lost a finger dicing onions as he watched.

We howled. I hadn't felt this great in weeks.

Parker must have seen the change in my face. She sipped her Chardonnay and said, "The apartment gleamed when I got in this morning. All the towels were laundered. Did you have a flash of guilt from my note or something?"

I practically choked on my cheesecake. Was I that obvious?

Parker chuckled. "I know you too well, Sam. My confident, bubbly college roommate just hasn't been herself, lately."

I gulped a mouthful of wine.

"Is everything okay at work?"

I answered, "Work? Work's terrific. I'm doing some great research for the firm and starting to get noticed."

"Then, why so glum? Alan?"

So, I told her. Yeah, I was lonely, but that wasn't my true problem. I told her about the credit card debt, the challenge of the extra 401(k) deductions from my paycheck, and how going to Barbachine practically bankrupted me. I didn't think I could make it in the city after all.

She poured more wine into both our goblets.

To my surprise she told me she'd been in exactly the same position when she first started out. Then she said that awful "B" word … "What you need, Samantha Davis is a budget."

I crossed my fingers to ward off vampire evil, but she wasn't kidding. She said if I wanted to run with the big dogs, I'd have to listen to her. So, she gave me homework. She said I had to write down every cent I spent—honestly—and she'd help me structure a budget.

Then, she reached for the bill, pulled cash from her wallet and paid for dinner.

I really love that girl.

So, instead of having lunch the next day, I sat at my desk and worked out my expenses. Here's what I found:

Samantha's Original Monthly Budget

Monthly income:	*$2791.14*

Rent:	*$1050*
Utilities	
Electric	*55*
Cable & High speed internet	*75*
Cell Phone	*102*
Land Line Phone	*15*

Dry Cleaning	45	
Laundry	25	
Manicures (1xperweek @ 12)	48	
Pedicure (once a month)	28	
Waxing	10	
Facial	55	
Hair Salon (4x per year @ 160)	54	
Taxis	325	
Food (guesstimate)	400	
Dining Out (guesstimate)	250	
Lunch ($5 per day during the week only)	105	
Health Club	100	
Coffee & Bagel before work	48	
Money owed to Dad	100	
Total	$2890	-$98.86
Extras:		
Clothes	200	
Vacations	100	
Visits to Parents	50	
Charities (parties)	25	
Total with Extras:	$3265	-$473.86

Well, no wonder I was sinking fast. Negative $473.86 per month!!! Now, how was I going to get four hundred and seventy-three dollars and eighty-six cents out of my budget? I already listed next to nothing for clothes! I guess I could walk to work and cut out the health club. I resisted the urge to crumple and toss the paper. Instead, I folded it neatly into quarters. I slid it into my purse, hoping the numbers would miraculously turn positive before I presented them to Parker tonight.

I headed to the break room for a cup of coffee.

After all, that was free.

I came home bearing Pizza with extra cheese. I wanted to thank Parker for dinner last night, and buy a little more time before she saw my indecent cash flow and really threw me out for good. But, Parker, saint that she is, pulled a bottle of Chianti from the cupboard eager as usual to set my finances straight.

"Let's see how your budget worked out," she said holding out an open hand.

I unfolded the paper and handed it to her. She chewed busily while reading my sheet as if it was the New York Times.

"Whoa. No wonder you're floundering. This is going to be tricky."

I was doomed, and said so.

She looked surprised. "No, Sam. This is do-able."

"You're kidding?"

"You're lucky you don't have a college loan to repay." She sipped her Chianti. "Most people our age do, and they really have to be careful with their money."

She reached for a pencil. "Look. You can skip the health club and use the gym downstairs. It's nothing fancy, but does the trick. That cuts one hundred bucks."

I already decided walking to work would be good exercise. She reminded me that running in Central Park, one of my more enjoyable past-times, was free. The kickboxing class I wanted would have to wait, though.

I saw her finger touch the Laundry entry and suggested I could hand wash most everything and would only dry clean what's necessary. That knocked another forty five dollars off the list.

Then, her gaze hardened. She said, "What about the cabs? That's $325 of your money."

I rolled my eyes. Upwardly mobile babes didn't take the bus. Would I be reduced to subways?

A dastardly gleam lit her eye as if she read my thoughts.

"You could make taking the bus look trendy wearing funky hats, white gloves and vintage sunglasses. Everyone will wonder who you are!"

I howled. I Love Lucy in disguise! That would be the day.

I wiped a tear from my eyes and chomped pizza if only to swallow the lump rising in my throat. Could I stick to a budget? I swiped perspiration from my upper lip with my napkin and took another sip of Chianti. Bless Parker and her wine.

Parker tallied up the adjusted numbers. Two hundred seventy dollars. Not even close! Her pencil stopped at the Cell Phone entry. She was sure I was paying way too much for my cell phone. A new plan would knock at least sixty bucks off the amount.

We decided the manicure and pedicures were a must, but the facials could go. That saved another $55.

I suggested we ditch the high speed Internet to save another $75. But, Parker said no. She wanted to keep it, so she offered to pay. Bless the girl, a million times.

We were now down to eliminating $13.86. A wicked grin crossed her face as she slashed $50 from my clothing money. I sent a prayer skywards. Maybe Versace would hear me.

My new budget looked like this:

Samantha's Revised Monthly Budget

Monthly income: *$2791.14*

Rent:	*$1050*
Utilities	
Electric	*55*
Cable	*25*
Cell Phone	*62*
Land Line Phone	*15*
Dry Cleaning	*35*

Laundry	*15*
Manicures (1x per week @12)	*48*
Pedicure (once a month)	*28*
Waxing (once every two months)	*20*
Hair Salon (4x per year @ 160)	*54*
Taxi's	*160*
Bus & subway fares	*50*
Food	*400*
Dining Out	*250*
Lunch ($5 per day during the week only)	*105*
Coffee & Bagel before work	*48*
Money owed to Dad	*100*
Total	*$2520* *+$271.14*

Extras:

Clothes	*$150 Life isn't so bad!*
Vacations	*$100 Cancun here I come!*
Visits to Parents	*They'll have to fund trip.*
Charities (parties)	*$21.14 It's not much!*

Wish List: *forget the wish list for awhile*

TIP: College loans can really put you behind the financial planning eight ball, but having a degree is well worth the extra burden. If you haven't finished college yet, or want an advanced degree, land a job that will pay your tuition. LOTS of major corporations do this. Even if you have to take a position below what you deserve, getting in on the ground floor of where you want to be is worth the trade-off for financial assistance in obtaining a college degree!

Parker and I toasted each other. We'd done it: A perfect budget with two hundred and seventy some-odd dollars for me to spend on extras. Now the real challenge is sticking to the numbers. This would be tricky since I could blow my entire monthly dining-out budget in one meal. Guess this was going to be part and parcel to the new me.

We were feeling pretty good at this point between the wine, the pizza and my budget in the black. But, Parker wasn't finished with me, yet. She quoted the financial wisdom by which she was living:

"Remember this, Sam. Live! Be smart with your money. You work hard for it and have it work hard for you! If you do this—soon you'll be able to have everything you want."

For the next month, I promised Parker to write down every penny I spent. To my surprise, rather than feeling hobbled by a budget, I felt exhilarated for finally getting a handle on my expenses. I glanced around our pristine apartment and grinned at Parker. I'd done it. I'd given myself personal satisfaction for the sheer joy of it. But best of all, I'd taken another dose of financial pleasure … and wanted more!

I bought myself a small notebook and started a budget journal. I've enclosed pages for you, too. You'll be surprised how focused your financial goals become!

YOUR BUDGET AND SAMANTHA'S BUDGET—RIGHT NOW!!

Monthly income:	**yours: $**	$2791.14
Rent:	**yours: $**	$1050.00
Utilities		
Electric	**yours: $**	$ 55.00
Cable & High speed internet	**yours: $**	$ 75.00
Cell Phone	**yours: $**	$ 102.00
Land Line Phone	**yours: $**	$ 15.00
Dry Cleaning	**yours: $**	$ 45.00
Laundry	**yours: $**	$ 25.00
Manicures (1x week @ 12)	**yours: $**	$ 48.00
Pedicure (once a month)	**yours: $**	$ 28.00
Waxing	**yours: $**	$ 10.00
Facial	**yours: $**	$ 55.00
Hair Salon (4x per year @ 160)	**yours: $**	$ 54.00
Taxis	**yours: $**	$ 325.00
Car Expenses (include insurance & gas)	**yours: $**	$__0
Food (guesstimate)	**yours: $**	$ 400.00
Dining Out (guesstimate)	**yours: $**	$ 250.00
Lunch ($5 per day during the week only)	**yours: $**	$ 105.00
Coffee & Bagel before work	**yours: $**	$ 48.00
Health Club	**yours: $**	$ 100.00
Money owed to Dad	**yours: $**	$ 100.00

Other	yours: $	$ 0
Other	yours: $	$ 0

Total	**Your Total: $**	$2890.00

Your Total Plus or Minus: $

    —

-**$98.86**

Extras:		
Clothes	yours: $	$ 200.00
Vacations	yours: $	$ 100.00
Visits to Parents	yours: $	$ 50.00
Charities (parties)	yours: $	$ 25.00
Wish List:	yours:	a new watch

Total with Extras:	yours: $	-$3265.00

Your Total Plus or Minus with Extras: $**   -**$ 473.86

DAILY EXPENSES FOR WEEK ONE
*REMEMBER WRITE DOWN EVERYTHING! It is for your eyes only …

Monday:

Tuesday:

Wednesday:

Thursday:

Friday:

Saturday:

Sunday:

DAILY EXPENSES FOR WEEK TWO
*REMEMBER WRITE DOWN EVERYTHING!

**Monday:**

**Tuesday:**

**Wednesday:**

**Thursday:**

**Friday:**

**Saturday:**

**Sunday:**

DAILY EXPENSES FOR WEEK THREE
*REMEMBER WRITE DOWN EVERYTHING!

Monday:

Tuesday:

Wednesday:

Thursday:

Friday:

Saturday:

Sunday:

DAILY EXPENSES FOR WEEK FOUR
*REMEMBER WRITE DOWN EVERYTHING!

Monday:

Tuesday:

Wednesday:

Thursday:

Friday:

Saturday:

Sunday:

DAILY EXPENSES FOR WEEK FIVE
(or until end of month)
*REMEMBER WRITE DOWN EVERYTHING!

Monday:

Tuesday:

Wednesday:

Thursday:

Friday:

Saturday:

Sunday:

Samantha's and Your Revised Monthly budget

Monthly income:	yours: $	$2791.14
Rent:	yours: $	$1050.00
Utilities		
Electric	yours: $	$ 55.00
Cable	yours: $	$ 25.00
Cell Phone	yours: $	$ 62.00
Land Line Phone	yours: $	$ 15.00
Dry Cleaning	yours: $	$ 35.00
Laundry	yours: $	$ 15.00
Manicures (1x per week @12)	yours: $	$ 48.00
Pedicure (once a month)	yours: $	$ 28.00
Waxing (once every two months)	yours: $	$ 20.00
Hair Salon (4x per year @ 160)	yours: $	$ 54.00
Taxis	yours: $	$ 160.00
Bus & subway fares	yours: $	$ 50.00
Food	yours: $	$ 400.00
Dining Out	yours: $	$ 250.00
Lunch ($5 per day during the week only)	yours: $	$ 105.00
Coffee & Bagel before work	yours: $	$ 48.00
Money owed to Dad	yours: $	$ 100.00
Other	yours: $	$ 0

Other   yours: $ $ 0

Total   yours: $ $2520.00
   Your Total: $ +$ 271.14

Extras:

Clothes   yours: $ $150 Life isn't so bad!
Vacations   yours: $ $100 Cancun here I come!
Visits to Parents   yours: $ They'll have to fund trip!
Charities (parties) yours: $ 21.14 It's not much!

Wish List: yours: $ Forget the wish list for
                                     awhile.

Go to: www.flirtingwithfinances.com today to order your workbook.

11

The next major distraction from my finance addiction was an older, extremely handsome, very rich man. It's not what you think. Well, then yes, I guess it is. But, I swear I didn't fall as bad as Aunt Sally. She totaled her life. Me? A few bumps and scrapes— maybe could have used a cast to re-set my brain!

It all started because of my new budget.

Walking up Madison Avenue, checking out the window displays and knowing I only had two hundred and seventy one dollars free for spending each month was pure hell.

In New York, that small change couldn't buy a designer pretzel.

So, like any good recovering shop-a-holic, I strolled from window to window and drooled. There were only two more blocks to the bus stop. I needed to head home because the sales wouldn't start for another month.

I was so caught up in the melancholy of the moment that the bourbon-smooth "hello" close to my ear didn't register at first. When the 'hello' finally did register, I quickly discovered it came from a grin that blended beautifully with this tanned, angular face, a pair of laughing blue eyes beneath longish, styled, salt-n-pepper hair. This very distinguished, sexy man wore a hand tailored, pin-stripe suit and blue tie.

So, I said, "Are you speaking to me?"

He nodded. "Carrying the weight of the world, are you? Is life so horrible?"

He spoke with a British accent to die for. I stared at him, speechless.

He chuckled. "Turn around, let me fix your shoulders." He turned my back to him.

I twisted out of his grasp. This guy set my stranger radar off the charts.

He laughed, turning my back to him again. "Don't be silly. I'm harmless. You look way too tense to ignore."

And, you know what? He knew exactly what to do. He used very firm pressure into the exact muscles where, to my amazement, tension gripped my neck like lion's teeth. The heat of his hands offered immediate relief. I couldn't have resisted if I tried. I wanted to melt into a puddle at his feet.

So, I did what any self-respecting woman smitten on sight would do. I pulled away. After all, that was the absolute weirdest thing I'd ever done on a city street.

I said to him, "You're a complete stranger. Thank you very much, but that's quite enough."

And, I lost all reason from there.

We shook hands. He was Christopher Steinberg. He lived on 78th. I told him my name and that I lived 79th. We walked the rest of the way. I told him way too much about myself. He told me nothing about himself. And then he asked for my business card, and invited me to a party at his house on Thursday. This was Tuesday. Holy Smokes.

Red Tulips arrived at the office the next day. The enclosed card said he was glad to have met me, confirmed the invitation to his party and invited a friend to join me. Morgan just happened to walk by and notice the tulips. So, I invited her. Guess what? She knew Christopher Steinberg.

Actually, THE Christopher Steinberg was considered one of the most eligible bachelors in the city. Not only did he come from wealth, he managed the portfolios of some very important families. EVERY woman considered Christopher a charmer, and willingly so.

She warned me not to get involved with him, because he was a confirmed bachelor. However, she would most certainly join me for the party. She wouldn't miss it for the world!

This was very, very cool.

On Thursday, completely in control—of my finances, at least, I limited shopping to my own closet. Stella McCartney and the Jimmy Choos debuted once more. I felt great. Especially because I hadn't violated my budget.

Yet.

Oh, wait. You'll see.

A silent, suited butler answered the door to Christopher's spectacular home. Class. Sophistication. The very air about the place whispered mountains of money. The curling, marble staircase reminded me of the love scene between Pierce Brosnan and Rene Russo wearing that painted on, black lace number in the movie, The Thomas Crown Affair.

Christopher's home was doing strange things to my libido.

He spotted us immediately. I introduced Morgan. He shook her hand. He kissed me, his lips lingering just a tad too long against my cheek. I inhaled his warm cologne, feeling like Alice about to tumble down the rabbit hole. He took my hand, admiring my Stella McCartney dress with eyes that said it all.

A proprietary gleam lit his eyes. "Sam, you look ravishing."

I wrapped his compliment around me like a mink. Smiling, I said, "Thank you" and sipped my champagne.

I motioned to the living room filled with gorgeous people. "Looks like the entire city accepted your invitation."

He surveyed the crowd. "Everyone came." His gaze held mine. "I wish I could spend more time with you this evening."

I waved a dismissing hand. "I understand. The host must mingle."

"Oh, it's not that. I have to leave town on unexpected business." He glanced at his Rolex. "In about twenty minutes, to be exact."

I rested my hand on his sleeve. "We just stopped in to say hello. Not to worry."

He leaned closer. "Will you have dinner with me next week?"

I almost choked on the champagne. Morgan covered her grin with a napkin. He seemed amused at my surprise. I recovered enough to see the sincerity in his gaze. He had beautiful, blue eyes. I'm a sucker for beautiful, blue eyes.

I told him he could call me on Monday and we'd set a date.

He checked his watch then kissed me on the cheek once more. My skin tingled where his lips touched.

"Stay, enjoy yourselves. I'm going to have to say good bye to the others."

I watched him work the room and knew I'd fallen head over heels. I was doomed. I hadn't felt drawn to a man like this since Alan. He was elegant, disarming and fun. Cultivating his attention intrigued me. Then, one thought hit. He had to be a good fifteen years older.

I said as much to Morgan.

"And the problem is? Age might have made a difference in the school yard, Sam, but not now."

She picked another pastry puff from a passing waiter, popping it between her tawny, glossed lips. "Look what he's done with his money. You could learn from him, Sam."

I said, "My Grandpa Wallace had a money manager, but he could never afford a house like this."

Morgan gave me her I'm-about-to-tell-you important-information look. "Sam, there are many different types of money managers."

I could feel her gearing up for a lecture and braced myself.

"The term money manager is generic for anyone who manages money, but the primary difference comes with the amount of money they manage and for how many clients. Some will manage the money for only one very wealthy person and will do all aspects from real estate to trusts to stocks, bonds, hedge funds, etc. But, a person who manages a hedge fund only is also referred to as a money manager. Some Financial Advisors (which is typically associated with working at a 'wire house', i.e. Morgan Stanley, UBS,

etc.) will call themselves money managers. In Christopher's case, however, he manages the money for two very wealthy individuals. He is paid one percent of the money under management and 20 percent of the profits."

I was shocked at how much she knew about managing money, especially Christopher's role in it, and said as much.

She grinned. "I had lunch with the right person yesterday. You will, too, once you get the knack of picking someone's brain for information." She laughed. "Most folks call it networking."

So Christopher worked for only two people. Since he had to leave his own party, two clients must be demanding enough.

Morgan wasn't finished explaining. *"There are lots of different roles in the financial world. Sometimes people will just use the easy generic phrase 'money manager,' but their roles vary."*

I took another sip of salvation bubbling in my glass just to shore myself up for the onslaught. Morgan positively glows when she taps those brain cells of hers. I wanted to understand what she had to say. I watched in admiration as she continued.

"'Financial Advisor' or 'Planner' will usually mean a person who develops an investment (or financial plan) for individuals, families and small companies. Grandpa Wallace called his advisor a money manager. Remember?"

I nodded. That was an easy question.

"This person's role includes examining the client's financial situation, including goals and time horizons to determine retirement planning, college planning, general investments and anything needed to complete the plan. They typically work for a wire house such as Schwab, TD Ameritrade, Morgan Stanley, UBS, etc. They are also required to hold certain licenses, such as a series 7, 63, and 65 which are issued by the SEC and FINRA. You can search each advisor's history at <u>www.finra. org</u>, which is the largest non-governmental regulator for all securities firms doing business in the United States."

I made a mental note to look up Christopher's information. I wondered if his 7, 63, 65 would be attracted to my 34-22-33. Ha! I pushed that thought away to concentrate on Morgan. I asked, "So, what's the best type of Advisor?"

"Good question. *The best way to determine a better educated Financial Advisor is to look for one who holds a recognized designation of "Certified Financial Planner" (CFP) which involves completion of a lengthy program and adherence to a strict "code of ethics."*

I said, "That sounds grueling."

"Yes, but incredibly reliable. Now, listen up, Sam. I'm not through."

I rolled my eyes and said, "Wouldn't you rather mingle?"

She lifted two more canapés from a passing tray. "Here, eat and listen."

She popped one into her mouth, taking the time to savor the incredible cheese flavor before continuing.

"*Now, stock brokers are individuals who are licensed to buy or sell financial securities. This was once a very lucrative business, but with the advent of the Internet and discount stock trading, the job has become archaic.*"

My gaze drifted to Christopher shaking hands with several guys who looked like rock stars. He seemed to know everybody.

"There's more Sam. Listen."

I met her gaze. I knew this was important, especially if I wanted to understand Christopher. I'd blown it once with Alan by not understanding his business world. I wasn't about to fail again.

"*Mutual Fund Salespersons are licensed to sell mutual funds only. They are required to have a series 6 license. They cannot sell stocks or bonds, and they usually work in banks.*"

I answered, "Mutual funds only. Got it."

"*Now, an Investment Analyst is someone who analyzes financial data and makes investment recommendations. An Equity Analyst analyzes stocks and stock issuers. A Credit Analyst analyzes bonds and bond issuers.*"

I held up a stopping hand as if trying to stop a freight train. I said, "Information overload. Warning! Warning!"

Morgan laughed. "Well, I'm almost done. And here's the good part."

I leaned forward. "It pertains to Christopher?"

She sipped her champagne, clearly delighted with its flavor. "Yes, it pertains to Christopher's area because he is a money manager. He only has two clients, but most will have more clients."

I grinned. "Well, then I'm like one big ear."

She lowered her voice. *"Like Christopher, an Investment Manager, Money Manager, or Portfolio Manager is someone who manages investment portfolios. They manage money for an individual or dozens of people, like a pool of mutual fund investors. An investment manager may work for large financial institutions like a bank, life insurance or trust company, managing its portfolio or providing management directly to third-party clients. "*

"Wow. So, there are times when an Investment Manager won't even know their clients."

She nodded, sipped more champagne. "Right. *Managing portfolios without requiring client approval for actions is called 'discretionary' money management which means that the Investment Manager will manage the portfolio independently, according to an established investment policy. Money or Investment Managers that most people are familiar with are mutual fund managers who have 'discretion' over the funds. So, the Money Managers running your 401(k) retirement plan are discretionary managers."*

She released a long breath. "There, I'm done."

I thought my cheeks would break from grinning. I understood every word she said. Now, I just hoped to remember it all in the morning.

To my absolute pleasure, Christopher and I dated steadily for the next two months. Twice a week, he picked me up in a limo or had the limo retrieve me. Then, one evening he pulled me against him in the limo, a gleam in his eye.

"The forecast is calling for snow this weekend. Let's fly to my family's villa in St. Bart's. We'll have it all to ourselves."

Characteristic of my classy behavior, my jaw dropped. Christopher all to myself in a villa under the warm, Caribbean sun! How incredibly romantic. This would take our relationship to a new level. Of course,

I wanted go. But, reality jerked me to a stop. Could I afford the trip with only two hundred and seventy something dollars to spare?

I sucked in one huge breath, looked him straight in the eye and said, "Let me see if I can get Friday off."

My boss and Morgan caught me by the coffee pot like avenging angels. We'd developed enough of a rapport by now to voice opinions on each other's personal affairs.

Chuck shook his head. "You can have Friday off, Samantha, but Chris Steinberg is a playboy. Do you know what you're getting into?"

I grinned, not believing a word he said. Christopher seemed way too sincere. "Yeah, isn't it great?"

Morgan groaned. "You only date the man twice a week. You have no idea what he does on the nights you don't see him."

I met her scrutiny. "I'm not falling in love with him, or anything." (I should have ducked in case lightning struck me.)

She harrumphed, crossing her arms across her chest. "Sam, have fun on St. Bart's, but pay attention to the facts."

I gazed down my nose at her and said, "I trust him."

Chuck snorted his amusement. "Well, don't go getting any permanent ideas about him."

I wanted to smack him for the direct hit. Dating Christopher was like dating American royalty.

I pointed a finger at Chuck. "Would you turn down a date with someone as charming as say, Prince William?

He frowned. "I'm a guy, Sam. Think of another question."

Staring at Chuck, it occurred to me I was head-over-heels for Christopher. I scoffed. "Do you think I'm a fool? This is just a fun weekend. It's Saint Barthelemy!"

Chuck shook his head and walked away. "I'll get Bonnie to cover for you."

Morgan wouldn't let me off the hook so easily. "Let's step away from the heady feelings, Sam. What about your budget? Christopher's not going to pay for everything, you know. I said learn from the man, not try to match him dollar for dollar. "

I swallowed hard. She was right, but I'd already accepted my fate. Manicure. Waxing. New bathing suit. Outfit for dinner. Sandals. And, of course, a spa tan. I was screwed.

I smiled. "It'll be worth it, Morgan. Trust me."

12

Would I ever learn?

We had the vacation from heaven. No one in that great big villa except an occasional servant. We watched the sun setting over the Caribbean Sea reflecting an azure blue across the infinity pool which was flanked by marble columns and climbing vines. I never believed such tranquility existed. Best of all, I held Christopher's undivided attention.

Only one fact haunted me through this magical Caribbean get-away. Christopher would return to his rich life, totally unscathed by this vacation. I, on the other hand, would be stone-cold poor. Even though it seemed to Christopher he paid for everything, this trip cost me $805.65.

I already blew my budget for the year!

My conscience gnawed at me as we toasted … my wine to his Evian, on our last night.

Was my personal investment in turning Christopher's head worth going broke? He'd never know how much this vacation left me in debt, but I certainly did. The truth invaded my balmy, tropical evening like a bucket of ice-cold water. Suddenly, the nectar in my glass didn't taste so sweet.

Cost of My Trip with Christopher:

Spa Manicure:	$22
Spa Pedicure:	$44
Bikini Wax:	$43
Facial:	$54
Waterproof Makeup:	$78.63
Spa Tan:	$75
New Outfit:	$194.54
Sandals:	$54.96
Bathing Suit w/Cover Up:	$239.52
SAMANTHA'S COST:	$805.65

The real kicker here is that the glow of the vacation faded way before my spa tan. Two days later, while strolling down Madison Avenue, I expected to meet Christopher on his walk home from work when what do I spy?

Damn him.

Far enough down the block, I saw Christopher's limo pull up to the sidewalk. I thought he saw me and was stopping, so I picked up my stride. But, no. I halted dead in my tracks. Christopher steps out, stops a woman who had passed me earlier when I lingered to gaze into a store window. This woman caught my eye because of her beauty. She was tall, leggy and gorgeous, with a mane of blond hair falling down to her elbows. The gold in her hair matched her close-cropped, shearling jacket. Tight, Nicole Miller jeans melted into a pair of leather and sheepskin boots hugging her legs right up to her knees. She looked sophisticated, casual and seductive. Any man would approach her—if he could swallow the lump in his throat to speak.

She had passed me with the easy step of a runway model. I couldn't help but admire her confidence. Now, my stomach knotted as she beamed at Christopher. They kissed, clearly familiar with each other. A groan of agony escaped my lips. He gestured to his limo. I could feel the heat of his proprietary hand on her back, just as I had felt it on mine countless times.

The son of a bitch.

My blood ran colder than the cloud of breath escaping my mouth as she entered the limo.

Chuck's words came back to me. "Christopher Steinberg is a playboy."

What was I thinking?

This man could have any woman, any time. And, he can't make a commitment!

My heart pounded in my ears. I was mortified.

And in debt doo-doo up to my ears.

I just stood there and watched the limo pull away.

He had never lied to me. Never committed. He had just been Christopher.

I cried all the way home. Beating myself up for never asking him for monogamy.

Stupidity was a hard nut to swallow.

Parker, of course, only shook her head when I told her. She reached across the mountain of bills between us on the tiny kitchen counter and squeezed my hand.

"Consider this a learning curve, Sam. Maybe if you visit Aunt Sally, you might find you got off easy."

So, I did—and learned that Parker was spot-on correct.

Not only did Aunt Sally get dumped after eighteen years and no commitment from a man of mega-wealth proportions whose family she came to know intimately, but she squandered two hundred and fifty thousand dollars he gave her as, um, pay off for giving him the best years of her young life (my words, not hers).

She showed me her closet filled with expensive and now vintage couture, accessories and two, maybe three hundred pairs of polished shoes, gleaming boots, and strappy sandals. Many of the shoes had magnificent beads and baubles. The colors swirled together like a Monet water color screaming: "Try us on"!!

And you know what? She didn't wear much of them anymore. The clothing and footwear stood as a monument to her stupidity. In comparison, with my one expensive Stella McCartney dress, the Choo shoes and my expenses for St. Bart's accredited to my financial failings, I got away with murder.

But I got the message: *A woman should plan her financial goals, and protect them at all costs.*

Those words rang in my ears all the way home. What irked me was that I knew this! A man could be the downfall to a woman's financial freedom (and a woman could be the downfall to a man's financial freedom too). The very same thought hit me the last time I visited Aunt Sally. How did I lose control—not only of myself, but of my finances? Had I been too embarrassed to admit to Christopher that I couldn't afford to go to St. Bart's? Or too vain to skip the spa tan and new bathing suit?

Damn.

I had betrayed my finances for emotions. Women are notorious for that one flaw.

I thought I was in love, but I was seduced by the man and his cash-ola. The fault was mine, not his. I'd made another mistake for the learning curve. Eating crow is not my favorite dish. But, I wear big girl panties, now. I can own this one. (I'm not happy to tell you that I still hadn't learned my lesson … or succumbed to my finance addiction, yet. But, that's for a later lesson.)

At work, I never told Morgan or Chuck why my feelings toward Christopher changed. I told them that Christopher was great fun, but way too expensive for me. Whether they believed me or not, I'll never know. I could care less. I had played the fool.

First Alan. Then Christopher. Two strikes. Flirting shook my emotional world one more time, and my romance roller coaster had truly affected my finances.

I needed a change. No more bimbo, flunky times for me!

I know. I'd find a new job that paid more and had better benefits.

13

For years I dreamed of being a lawyer. My entire time at college was centered around this goal. But, even with all those interesting cases I worked on, the truth hit me like a commuter train: I'd had enough of the legal world.

I didn't want to pay the dues of three more years before finally seeing the inside of a court room—if only to accompany an attorney. My work week had evolved into sixty five hours. Every other Saturday found me in the office. Don't get me wrong, I didn't mind the long hours. It's what a girl does to get ahead. But, long hours and massive amount of detailed readings just weren't for me. I realized if I truly was dedicated, I wouldn't mind the grind.

But, I did.

I was tired. My budget was tight, and it would be years before I could afford the killer outfits the female lawyers wear to court. I needed some immediate gratification to boost my flailing ego. It was tough to admit I wasn't cut out to be in law.

But, no sooner had I closed that door in my mind than the proverbial window opened. The placement agency I had contacted called with a job I could not refuse. The successful computer software designer, Manfredi Mozel, needed a marketing assistant. The position was designed as a training program for international sales, and I could achieve that in a year. I certainly liked technology. My fingers itched at the prospect. The idea of traveling the world, participating in computer shows and setting trends, sent a thrill through me.

And, the salary started at $86,500.

This had to be kismet. I felt a tad guilty receiving this call at work, but hey, we can take personal calls now and again. I ran into the ladies room and gave myself a high-five in the mirror. This opportunity was too cool to ignore. Change was exciting after all!

By week's end, I sat in the personnel office trying not to dwell on the fact that this company gave me my first break. I consoled myself thinking that if Dad were alive, he would cheer the career switch. Taking risks, and all that jazz.

My musings were interrupted by good old, reliable Penny Pincher. She sat in front of her computer looking at my records.

She tapped the screen. *"Samantha, it's really important that you decide what to do with your 401(k). You have two options:*

One, move the 401(k) to an Individual Retirement Account, commonly called an IRA. This, and all IRAs, are retirement plans created by the US Government to enable people to save tax-deferred (i.e., pay taxes later) for their retirement, under section 408 of the Internal Revenue Code. A person can start taking the money out at 59 ½ and there are rules on the distribution of monies. (We'll get into these at a later time).

She continued. "Since you're moving to another company, the type of IRA you would choose is called a Direct Rollover IRA, because you're directly rolling over your 401(k) into this plan. You don't have any other IRAs, so you would be eligible to move this IRA into another company sponsored retirement plan in the future. However, if you did have another IRA, or if you contributed to the Direct Rollover IRA, you would not be eligible to move it to another company sponsored retirement plan.

I said, "Okay. *What's my second option?"*

She lifted a well-shaped brow. *"Second, you could take a payout by check. The Internal Revenue Service (IRS) will charge you an early withdrawal, also called a withholding penalty, of 20%. This money would be taxable at your current rate of 28%. So, it is not worth taking your money out unless you're really desperate.*

I had to think for a moment. Was I desperate? Not yet! Yahoo.

Penny continued. *"Some companies will allow you to leave the retirement plan in place, even though you're no longer working there. Unfortunately our plan does not offer this option."* The Head of Personnel was very articulate about this subject. I guess they took quitting seriously.

She handed me a 401(k) disbursement instructions form. *"Once you've made the decision, fill out this form. Be sure the routing numbers are correct and mail it to the address below. You have 90 days. If the form hasn't been received in 90 days the company will sell your fund investments, and disburse the money to you. If this happens, they will withhold the governmental charges of 20% early withdrawal penalty and taxes, in your case an additional 28%. So you see, it's very important to protect your retirement account."*

Okay. I wanted to roll over my 401(k) into an Individual Retirement Account (IRA) because cashing out would cause all sorts of heartache in taxes and penalties. But, where, oh where, was I to go?

Penny suggested I search for companies offering IRAs on the Internet, but who could I trust? Grandpa Wallace had a stockbroker (now called a Financial Advisor), but he'd never be interested in managing my paltry savings. So, I hit the street.

I remembered a discount brokerage house (whatever that is!) down the block. So, I headed there. Once inside, there was no one to be seen. Did discount brokerage mean no advisors to consult? I laughed at my own joke and reached for a brochure on IRA vs. Roth IRA—taxes now, taxes later ... Sheesh. I hadn't a clue. I took the brochure and departed. No one knew I had even been there.

The next stop was my bank. The lovely woman who helped me with my credit card told me I could consider her my account manager at that bank.

I felt my nose scrunch in embarrassment. "I don't have much to invest, just what I've accumulated in my 401(k) over the past three years."

She smiled and said, "Every retirement account starts somewhere, Ms. Davis. Here." She handed me forms. "If you decide to move your retirement account here, please fill out these forms and either bring them back or mail them in. When the funds have transferred over we'll sit down and decide what investments are appropriate for you. In the meantime, can I answer any questions?"

Suddenly I felt protective of my tiny retirement sum. I could feel Aunt Sally's hand on my shoulder.

"I do have a couple of questions. *What is the return on your IRAs?*"

The woman smile again. Guess that was bank policy.

"There isn't one set of returns on an IRA. It varies, depending on what investments you choose."

I was stumped, but tried to look inquisitive. "I don't understand."

"Well, an IRA is a government plan which is really like an umbrella covering investment choices. You can invest in stocks and bonds. Most people invest in a selection of mutual funds, which are a combination of stocks, bonds and cash. So, once again, there isn't one set of returns, it varies depending on what investments you choose."

Oh, yeah, the foundation and makeup theory Morgan had told me about! Now, I was getting the hang of it.

"Are there any annual charges?"

She nodded, folding her hands on the desk. *"We charge $40.00 per year to manage the account, and a $75.00 closure fee if you move the account. Your statement will read, Bank of Northeastern USA, Custodian for Samantha Davis, IRA, as we are the holder of your account."*

"What do you need from me to open the account?" I was on a roll, feeling like I found a safe home for my money.

"We'll need information about your 401(k) plan including account number and balance, plan sponsor name, phone number and address ..."

I held up a stopping hand and rummaged in my bag. "Hold on a minute, let me write this down." She watched as I scribbled, 401(k) account number, balance, plan sponsor name, phone, addy ...

She continued. *"Also your past employer's name, phone and address, and your beneficiary's birth date and social security numbers."*

"Beneficiary?"

"Yes, the person to whom you wish to leave the IRA in case something happens to you."

"Hmm. I didn't think of a beneficiary."

She held up a finger of wisdom. *"And, it must be a person."*

Huh? I said, "What else would it be?"

The woman chuckled, leaning in. "I had a meeting this morning with a fellow who wanted to leave everything to his dog. Can you imagine? He was fighting with his family. Finally, he decided on a niece who was only three years old. So be sure you give me the name of a person."

I pulled the discount brokerage brochure out of my purse ready for some real explanations. Aunt Sally would be proud.

"This mentions a Roth IRA. What is it? And what are the differences between it and an IRA?"

"The differences basically have to do with the tax advantages. The simple explanation is a traditional IRA is taxed when the money is taken out (or distributed) and a Roth IRA is taxed when the money is put in (or contributed). Let's say you contribute $3000 to your traditional IRA. You can deduct this money from your income taxes for that year.* When you take the money out after age 59 ½, you will pay taxes on the money. If your tax bracket is lower this is advantageous."

[*for your exact deduction check with the IRS or an accountant.]

"In a Roth IRA you do not deduct the money from your income taxes and therefore have paid tax on the amount of the contribution. So, when you take the money out after age 59 ½ you do not have to pay taxes."

"In both cases, **you do have to pay taxes on any gains in the account above your initial investment.**

"So, in your case, Samantha, if you decide to move your 401(k) into a Roth IRA you would have to pay taxes on the amount already in the account. This amount will be taxed as ordinary income, which for you is 28%."

I had a lot to think about. The Roth seemed like a bad idea because I'd have to lose part of my initial principal investment. I pretty much decided to move my account to this highly professional woman at the bank, but I wanted to be sure. I shook her hand and returned the same smile she offered.

"Thank you for this information. I'm going to shop around a bit more, but will let you know my decision."

I stopped at four more banks and brokerage houses on the way home. That's the beauty of New York City: everything's at your fingertips!

By the time I arrived at the apartment I had enough brochures and forms to decimate a small forest. I almost choked the woman at the last brokerage house I visited. Nothing like a hard sell to open a retirement account to make a person look greedy. I didn't feel warm and fuzzy about my retirement in her hands!! All she could see was commissions on my investments. Yikes!

Check out the instructions and forms for IRA Rollovers on the Internet. All the investment houses have forms available: schwab.com, fidelity.com, and tdameritrade.com are really good sites. And, depending on the amount of the rollover, the investment firm might offer an incentive program (and we love 'free' money).

After looking at the material I gathered, and checking on the Internet - I returned to my bank. I already had my account and credit card with them. I felt I could trust their service.

My account manager tapped me on the hand after I handed her my filled out forms.

"Samantha, did you ask your new employer if you can roll this plan into their retirement plan? It not only could potentially save you fees, but your new company might give you a higher matching percentage rate."

Now, here was someone thinking on my behalf.

"I never thought to ask."

She smiled again. "I may work on commission, but I would highly recommend you explore that option before transferring your retirement account."

I left buzzing with the satisfaction of knowing my money would work for me. It felt good, too, that my account manager had pointed out an option I hadn't considered. My best interest was her primary concern.

Not bad.

As I walked home, the air smelled sweeter. I was a woman on a budget and managing my income. I was about to start a new job, in a new field with a higher paying salary. This financial well-being was a heady feeling … I could get addicted to it!

Meanwhile, my rumbling stomach reminded me it had been a long time since lunch. I wondered if Morgan would be free to meet me at Sophia's for pizza and a glass of wine. After all, I might have jilted the firm, but Morgan was my friend forever.

I reached for my cell phone, wondering what type of wildlife might be grazing at Sophia's tonight …

14

I never made it to Sophia's for pizza. A phone call from my mother had me on the next train home.

Grandpa Wallace died.

I felt like I'd been backhanded by a typhoon. My brain cells went on auto-pilot because what I'd done between the phone call and arriving at my mother's house felt unreal. In a fog, I scribbled a note for Parker, took a bus to the station, bought my ticket, wound through the jostling crowd, and found an empty seat on the train. I could have been on Mars. Nothing seemed familiar. Nothing registered. My head felt numb.

When I arrived home the taxi driver was kind enough not to notice my red eyes and runny nose, but my mother wasn't.

"Oh, Samantha, I shouldn't have told you over the phone."

I fell into my mother's arms and we rocked each other and cried. First Dad. Now, Grandpa. How would we live without them?

I slept away the entire next day after the funeral. Exhausted, I dragged myself back to the train and into the city on Tuesday. Thank goodness I didn't start my new job until after the weekend.

Morgan met me at Sophia's for pizza at seven. I told her about Grandpa Wallace's life and how he always said, "Life is short, Sam.

Enjoy every minute! Live for today, but plan for the future, and judge your wealth in terms of happiness not money."

We cheered him with a glass of Chianti by the bar while waiting for our table. Sophia's, the best pizza place in the city, was always packed. Life slowly seeped back into my bones as I watched the familiar world around me.

Or, it might have been the wine.

Morgan noticed. "Color's coming back into your cheeks." She smiled, and as always, her genuine concern warmed me.

"Life goes on, doesn't it?"

We touched goblets in a meaningful toast. I took a sip of my wine, still caught up in the funeral. I met Morgan's gaze. "Can you imagine? The neighbors started asking who was in line for Grandpa Wallace's inheritance."

Morgan grimaced. "Oh, that's ugly." She gently touched my arm. "Speaking about money, did you take care of your 401(k) rollover?"

Just like Morgan. Back to business.

"You'd be proud. I did my research and after talking with the woman at my bank, I transferred my 401(k) to my new job at Mozel."

She patted my shoulder. "Well done, Sammy."

I could have sworn the guy sitting at the bar behind me sat up, his ear pricked like a dog smelling a bone. I glanced at his back. Nice looking back. Big. Broad shoulders beneath a Tommy Bahama shirt. Blond hair. What-e-v-e-r.

But, he didn't turn. I must have been mistaken. Morgan met my gaze.

"He's not your type."

We clinked goblets again. "Your new job sounds exciting," she added.

A shiver ran down my spine at the prospect. "I'm thrilled at the opportunity. And the higher salary will really boost my cash flow."

Morgan's cell phone rang. She glanced at the number. "I have to take this call. I'll be right back."

While she stepped outside, I indulged in people watching. I turned to avoid getting smacked by a passing, oversized Prada bag.

Just as I turned, the guy from the bar stood and we bumped.
Smack. Splash.

Damn.

Red wine doused his yellow shirt.

"Shit! My new shirt!"

Did he just say that?

I said, "Oh, no! I'm so sorry!"

Our eyes clashed and his gaze turned from anger to fascination. I swear. I saw the change in those big brown eyes. His look sent a shot right down to my gut. Then again, I was one raw nerve from the funeral and thought maybe I was just too sensitive at the moment.

He was T-A-L-L and downright stunning. I'm sure I must have seen him on some soap opera or made-for-TV movie or something.

I stammered, "L-let ... let me get some club soda to clean your shirt."

He grabbed my hand. "It's okay. Don't worry about the shirt."

I shook my head. "I'm so embarrassed."

"It's my fault. I should have looked before I moved. I'm clumsy like that."

I laughed. "I don't think you have a clumsy bone in your body."

He grinned and I melted. I could feel it happening again. Another stranger and here I was turning into another puddle at his feet.

"At least let me buy you a drink," I said.

He seemed to think about that. He shrugged. "Okay, if you tell me your name."

I said, "Samantha. Samantha Davis."

"Keith Cunningham. I'll have a Jack and coke."

His grasp, warm as sable, curled around my hand. It was just a handshake, but his touch felt so darned intimate. I could feel the blush rise on my cheeks.

He ushered me into the seat he had just vacated. The wood still felt warm from his body. I ordered him a drink and more wine for me and Morgan.

Morgan gave me that I-can't-leave-you alone-for-a-minute look when she returned.

I ignored her. Keith was killer cute.

I introduced them. Morgan shook hands and quickly pulled away. Something about him disappointed her and it was clear on her face.

She asked, "Are you a native New Yorker?"

He grinned. I liked the heat of it.

"No. I'm from Portland. Been here a year. Trying to find my way in the Big Apple."

"What do you do?"

Didn't Morgan know that was a rude question to ask? But, I wanted to know, too, God bless her.

He looked sheepish. "I start a new job next week. Was selling real estate, but it's not for me."

A kindred spirit. I chirped up. "I know what you mean. I just left a great law firm after believing for so long that I wanted to be an attorney."

Morgan interrupted. "So where's your new job?"

"Goldman Sachs." Again, that killer grin.

I felt my eyebrows rise. "Nice."

His gaze bore into mine. "So, if you left your attorney career, are you out of work?"

I shook my head. "Oh, I couldn't afford that. I start a new job next week."

His shoulders squared just a little bit more. His eyes lit with interest.

"Where?"

Morgan rolled her eyes and tugged my sleeve. "Our table is ready, Sam."

I rose to leave. He caught my arm. "I'd love to take you to dinner one night."

I blinked. Did he just ask me out?

"Let's go, Sam," Morgan urged.

He was just too cute to ignore. I dug a card out of my bag. "Here's my old business card. The office number won't reach me, but the cell phone will."

He grinned again, saints be praised.

"I'll call you." His gaze lazily raked over us. "Nice meeting both of you. Enjoy your pizza."

Morgan propelled me away from the bar.

"He shakes hands like he's looking at you naked. I know a barracuda when I see one."

I was stunned. "What? He was charming."

We took our seats. She snapped her napkin with disgust and looked me dead in the eye. "This city is filled with gorgeous men. But, gorgeous men who are between jobs are dangerous. He's way too smooth. Didn't you shake hands with him?"

"Well, yes." And it set every nerve ending aquiver from my fingertips to my toes.

"Well?"

"Well, what? He's a hunk with a Type A personality. Eager. Attentive. Starting a job with a fabulous company. I'll bet he dances great, too."

She glanced at the menu. "Use your head, Sam. Be careful if he calls."

"'If'_is the magic word, Morgan."

She shook her head. "Oh, no. He'll call. We were talking money over there and he heard us."

I winced in disbelief. "You are so cynical."

"And you just lost your grandfather, and are still heartbroken. You're incredibly vulnerable right now. Please don't ignore that fact."

I gulped my wine. She was right. Again. Damn it.

"I don't want to think about it."

"Fine, Sam. Let's order. I'm starved."

I wanted to say she was starved for a man. But, I had to admire her. She was no pushover. I tried to keep the surly out of my voice.

"I'm going to dance naked in the street when you finally accept a date."

She arched an eyebrow. "Well, you can start peeling off that sexy pink sweater right now. I have a date Friday with a corporate attorney I met at Toastmasters."

My jaw dropped along with my menu. "No!"

She surveyed her menu like a queen. "Yes. I've had my eye on him for a year."

"A year?! Is he cute?"

She nodded, looking like the proverbial cat about to pounce the canary. "He's never going to know what hit him."

She laughed and I howled. God, I love this girl.

15

Keith Cunningham called the next day. We chatted for almost an hour. You'd think we'd been friends for life. He was thirty four, stood six feet two inches high and weighed in at 205 pounds of what I remembered as pure muscle. Born and raised in Portland, he had no siblings and his parents were divorced. Most of his free time, he spent working out. Humble about his looks, he laughed when I asked if he was ever on TV.

His new position at Goldman Sachs had something to do with distributions. Not wanting to sound financially wanting, I assumed he meant retirement accounts. So, I babbled on about how I just re-invested my 401(k) and had landed a new job with a starting salary over $86,000.

I mentally cringed. Morgan would kill me. But, it just fell out of my mouth.

"You'll be a rich woman in no time," he said with laughter in his voice.

I cradled the phone to my ear, tucking my feet between the cushions of the couch. "Well, if I stick to my budget, I'll do fine."

I congratulated myself for sounding so level headed. Something about him made me think he could care less if I shopped in Bloomie's basement.

"So, when can I take you to dinner?"

"Oh, let me get my calendar," I said, and tapped a finger to my chin.

"I'm not kidding. How about tomorrow?" He sounded hopeful.

"Where would we go?"

I could feel him grinning through the phone. "I'll surprise you."

The next night found me bawling like a baby. Gawd, I felt awful. Dressed for my date in a leather jacket, jeans and spiked boots, no matter how long I stared at myself in the mirror trying to calm my red eyes and blotched skin, I couldn't stop the tears.

Mom had called.

The doorman buzzed the apartment and informed me that Keith was getting impatient waiting for me. Whoa. Did we have a temper here?

I glanced at my watch. Oh, heavens. He'd been waiting twenty minutes. Shades of Alan rocked my memory. I couldn't do this to another date.

I looked like hell, but what else could I do? Keith had been so charming on the phone last night. Once I explained, he'd understand.

I stepped out of the elevator.

I watched his gaze switch from anger to concern. In three strides he was at my side, taking both my hands in his.

"You've been crying. What's the matter, Sam?"

Sam. Our first date and he was already calling me Sam. I liked that. Darn it all, tears filled my eyes again. I pressed my fingers against my mouth.

Keith walked me to the couch in the lobby.

"Here, sit down. Tell me what's wrong."

I wiped my eyes on the crumpled tissue in my hand. I said, "I didn't mean to keep you waiting. I got a phone call and it upset me. I didn't want you to see me looking like a blubbering idiot."

He chuckled. "Blubber away. This lobby's pretty nice. I didn't mind waiting. Now, what's wrong?"

I shook my head. "Nothing's wrong."

"Then why the tears?"

I indulged in a long, cleansing breath. "Remember I told you my grandfather died last week?"

He nodded. His big, brown puppy dog eyes watched mine.

"Well, apparently he left everything to me. I'm so mixed up inside. I'm thrilled to be his beneficiary, but just wish he was alive to keep it. It's so confusing. I don't know how to feel."

He put a strong, warm arm around me. His sandalwood aftershave overrode a mild, musty smell to his jacket. I concentrated on the heady feel of his large body next to mine.

"You're an heiress. You're one lucky lady. You should celebrate."

He pulled me to my feet, giving me a long, lazy once-over with his gaze.

"Let's go find a quiet place for dinner and you can tell me all about your phone call. I'll help in any way I can."

Dinner lasted all weekend. Keith stayed with me at the apartment until Parker came home. He was a perfect gentleman. Every once in a while he kissed me, but his kisses soothed and reassured—nothing like "I want to jump your bones" kisses. He promised to call me in the morning, and did. We spent the day outdoors. Carriage rides through the park, window shopping. I knew he wanted to distract me from my sadness. He touched my heart with his kindness. I hadn't had this kind of complete attention from any man—ever.

Sunday he took me to brunch and we pored over books on estate planning and investing. Keith was determined to help me handle my inheritance correctly. No one appreciated his concern more than I.

Morgan nearly clocked me with her coach bag when I told her on Monday night. "You told Keith what?"

I held a hand over my head to fend her off. "Come on. We're supposed to be celebrating my first day at work. I turned down a date with Keith to see you."

She huffed even more. "Tell me you didn't disclose your financial situation to that man."

Suddenly my new-found intimacy with Keith seemed ugly. I shook away the bad feeling. Morgan was dead wrong this time.

"There's chemistry between us. He's sincere. I trust him."

Morgan actually shook me. "Are you out of your mind? I warned you about him!"

"Well, you're wrong. He even brought me books on estate planning. He's no different than you in wanting to help me with my finances."

Her eyes narrowed to slits. "Has he tried to sleep with you?"

I felt righteous indignation saying, "Absolutely not. He's been a perfect gentleman."

She seemed to loosen up a bit. "Sam, promise me you'll be careful. You are so vulnerable right now."

The next few weeks were a whirlwind of phone calls by lawyers, accountants and the almighty Executor of the Estate.

The Executor of the Estate is the person who handles the administration of the estate: coordinating all assets of the deceased, paying unpaid bills, paying the taxes, and disbursing the remaining property. The Executor handles all of these general details. While Samantha was the sole heir, some of her Grandfather's personal effects and small sums of money were bequeathed to friends and people who touched her Grandfather's life. The Executor of the Estate handles details like these.

My new job was taking off. I loved every minute at work. And behind it all, Keith kept coming back for more. We saw each other almost every day after work and every weekend. His job at Goldman Sachs was moving right along. Come to think of it, I'm not sure of his title. But, he never pressured me to talk about finance, so I didn't pressure myself. If he would only stop kissing me until I melted I'd remember to ask him these questions. Sheesh. I'd become such a sucker for his kisses.

I discovered Keith was the best listener I had ever met. We talked about everything. When I expressed concern about aspects of my job, he talked me through them. When I spoke of Parker, his responses reflected my pride in my friend. If Grandpa Wallace came up, his sympathy was genuine. So, I showed him the estate portfolio to help hammer out the details. After all, someone who worked at Goldman Sachs certainly knew what he was doing.

He tapped the portfolio. "You should sell all the stocks and bonds and pay the taxes. That way, you'll have cash to do with as you need."

I could feel my brow crease. "That's a lot of money. I don't think I should do that."

He shook his head. "Honey, your grandfather was an older man. His investments reflect his age. This portfolio isn't geared for a beautiful, young woman like you. You need capital. What if you decide to buy a condo or something?"

Then he leaned over and kissed me until I couldn't think. Heaven help me. Oh, wait. I already was in heaven.

The Executor disagreed, saying that Grandpa Wallace's portfolio was very sound. He argued with me for quite some time. But I was the sole beneficiary and so in the end, he agreed to sell 85% of the stock portfolio.

Keith and I spent all of our free time together for the next four months. Every night after work. Every weekend. He was charming. Attentive. He was generous to a fault. Whenever we went out, he was quick to pull out his credit card and pay. He bought me silly gifts. A funky hat. Fudge. Flowers. A polar bear to hug when I couldn't hold him.

Parker and Keith finally met. She liked him, I think. She made a vague offer to double date with her boyfriend, Franco, sometime, but we both knew that would never happen with our opposing schedules.

I, however, was falling in love.

On our four month anniversary, Keith woke me at seven thirty in the morning. Not with a phone call, but buzzing my door. He flew into the apartment stopping long enough to take a full view of me in my pajamas and ankle socks. He grabbed my hand, pulling me down the hallway to my bed—since that was the closest thing, and all. He pushed me down by the shoulders to sit, knelt on one knee, then said, "Marry me."

I bolted to my feet. "What?"

He grabbed my hands in those mitts of his. "I've waited all my life for someone like you. Let's elope."

"You're serious." I couldn't believe my ears.

He cocked his head that funny way, looking sheepish but thrilled with himself. "I've booked a noon flight to Vegas. We have to leave now."

I began to sputter. "Keith … you're out of your mind!"

"No. Just in love, baby. Come on! It'll be a blast. Besides, Parker's moving out to live with Franco, and my lease is up. I can move right in." He tapped my nose. "We can save money on rent."

I shook my head. Was I dreaming? Alarms were blasting through my head, but I just repeated, "You want to get married?"

"More than anything in the world. Please say, yes." He kissed both my hands.

"But a wedding … my Mom … "

"We'll have a party when we return. Getting married is about you and me, not a million people."

His argument picked up steam, but really, he already hooked me at 'marry me.'

"Let's just sneak off. We can call work on Monday. I've already booked you a day at the Las Vegas Canyon Ranch Spa. We'll be back by Tuesday. Come on. Say, yes!"

My mind reeled. I held his gaze for a long time, letting my eyes roam over his chiseled features. Could I spend the rest of my life with this man? My insides quivered. My heart tattooed in my chest. He was everything a girl could want. Loving. Generous. Sexy. Attentive. Smart. This was way too exciting. Was my bikini in my purse?

I kissed him soundly on the lips, ignoring those tiny common sense police pounding on my logic and said, "Yes, I'll marry you, you crazy man! Let me dress."

16

I pinched myself. Every inch of me tingled at the hunger in his eyes. His hot, lingering kiss before he left me at the Canyon Ranch Spa carried me right to the massage table, through the manicure and pedicure and added to the glow from the most incredible facial I've ever experienced. I managed to glance at the bill before he snatched it from my hand. $540.

Wow.

We bought our wedding bands, then our wedding clothes. We chose our outfits by rating them with kisses. When my knees finally buckled, I was wearing a strapless silk number that hugged like a glove and reflected the clear blue sky above Las Vegas. Luckily, I had brought my Jimmy Choos. They matched perfectly.

Keith settled for an Armani linen shirt that set off his bronzed skin and golden hair. The shirt accentuated the muscles in his arms and back, just begging for my hand. His honey-colored slacks draped his hips in a 1950's Hollywood, baggy look. I could feel the heat of his body beneath the fabric. He was glorious. And in three short hours, he was going to be mine.

I liked the sound of Mrs. Keith Cunningham.

We stepped onto the sidewalk, our purchases in hand. There, parked at the curb stood a new Porsche. Keith pushed his parcels into my already crowded hands, not taking his eyes off the car.

"Wow, Samantha look at this Porsche! It's the most beautiful car I've ever seen!" He circled around the car tracing the form with the palm of his hand inches above the surface.

I laughed. "You're salivating, Mr. Cunningham!"

He gave me that lopsided grin I loved so much. "One day I'm going to get one of these babies. They're such a great investment, and the new advancements and innovations that Porsche engineers have done in the last year are light years ahead of the first 911."

He closed his eyes for a sacred moment, and said, "You don't drive the car, you become the car." He sighed. "I can see it now. You and I cruising through the countryside, top down, the wind blowing through our hair."

I bought into his fantasy. "We'll stop at Bed and Breakfasts and have hot, romantic weekends forever!"

He took his packages from me and kissed me hard. "One day, Babe, one day."

Our wedding was a bit hokey. The Las Vegas wedding chapel with an Elvis impersonator waiting in the back for the next couple took some of the meaning out of the moment. And, we chose to ignore that the best man and maid of honor were strangers! But, our honeymoon suite—and Keith's fine attention made up for the cheesy wedding. I have to say, I spent the most amazing night of my life in Keith's arms. Sensual, hot, steamy sex while gazing into each other's eyes was everything I believed romance was meant to be. I had finally found true love!

Back in New York, my mother's despair over our elopement broke my heart. I pondered her concerns as I climbed another landing of the dilapidated building that had been Keith's home before we married. No wonder he never invited me to his place. The stairs creaked, paint peeled off the walls and there was no air conditioning.

He had the good grace to be apologetic.

I shrugged, plastering a smile on my face that could have held the paint on the walls and said, "I don't mind, honey. Aunt Sally lives in a walk-up. It must have been difficult for you before the job at Goldman Sachs."

Keith opened his apartment door and I was floored. I can handle a struggling bachelor. I cannot handle piggish. I saw piggish. The floor hadn't been vacuumed in weeks. Dirty dishes looked like they were trying to climb out of their own way in the sink. They were fuzzy enough to be alive. A mountain of garbage sat like Jabba-the-Hut in the corner. A bucket between two unmade beds held old water from a rainstorm that leaked through the veins of blackened plaster in the ceiling.

But, worst of all, the musty, moldy smell pervading the apartment reminded me of the dank smell of his leather coat the night I learned I inherited Grandpa Wallace's estate. Keith had lived here long enough for his jacket to absorb the mildew. All I could hear was my mother's slightly shrill, hardly contained words circling around my head. "Well, of course I trust your judgment, dear. But, after four months, how well do you know this man?"

He blamed the mess on his roommate. I chose to believe him. Heaven help me. I had to.

We waited three more months for Grandpa Wallace's estate to settle. *After the house was sold, real estate agents paid, taxes paid, lawyers paid, executor paid and account balances paid, I received my inheritance.*

The real estate agent charged 6% to sell Grandpa's home, and that was $9,000. Unpaid income taxes for Grandpa's last year were $17,490.20 of the estate. The Executor charges 2% of the estate and that was $5,000. The lawyers, $7,500 more. Gifts to his friends totaled $32,000. Funeral expenses were $4,400. Brokerage fees to liquidate the stock and bond portfolio were $2,179.63. When it was all over I was left with $172,430.17. I was expecting $250,000, but for a 26 year old woman, I sure was grateful for what I got!

The estate executor wanted to wire the funds to my bank account, but I had to indulge my juvenile need to see the money in my hands. The executor reluctantly mailed me the check. Little did I know that the *interest amount of 2.5% on $172,430.17 equaled $4310.75 per year or $11.79 per day for every day I held the check in my hot little hand. In other words, until I deposited that money, I was losing the equivalent of a manicure a day! I really should have taken the executor's advice and wired the money instantly.*

Keith and I sat on the couch staring at the check. It felt great to have such a nest egg. I silently thanked Grandpa Wallace for taking care of me, one more time. I was reveling in my warm feelings when Keith said, "Let's pay off our credit card debt first."

I pulled out of my reverie. "How much do we owe?"

"Let's see." He pulled the statement from a file on the coffee table with the rest of our bills. "Looks like we owe $31,967.63."

You could have zapped me with a Tazer.

"What? How did we charge that much?" I tore the statement from his hand. Everything we had done in the past four months had been charged.

Keith shrugged. "It's the price of living, honey. Between the vacations, dining out, getting married, we just did."

I opened the credit card file and fished out the first bill. I swallowed a lump rising in my throat. Keith had a balance of almost $12,000 on the card before we met. "What about this $12,000? You charged that before we got married."

"What does that matter, now? We'll still have over a hundred and forty grand and a clean slate."

He began nuzzling my hair. "How about I pay off my balance in kind?" He trailed kisses down my neck with hot lips. The heat of his breath sent shivers down my spine. He whispered, "What will you charge me for loving you until you can't think? Can't move? Can't breathe? Will you let me, honey?"

By now, his hand was beneath my shirt doing wonderful things to my stomach and breasts. My heart thrummed in my chest. My husband had me trembling, already. Oh, hell. I could forgive him his debt in oh, say, maybe twenty years or so.

I giggled as his lips covered mine. I plunged my hands under his shirt, the velvet touch of skin over muscle teasing my fingertips. I pulled my mouth just far enough away to murmur, "How about you play boy-toy for the weekend to start chiseling down the debt?"

My voice became breathy from his knowledgeable hands. I cried out, "Oh, God, Keith, don't stop now!" And, promptly forgot what we had been discussing.

Time flew. Keith and I had been married for over four months. I couldn't remember ever being happier. My mother kept asking when we would have a party to celebrate, but Keith kept talking me out of one. But, really, he was right. Why spend $10,000 on a party when we had such a hit on the credit card debt? We'd wait. I had to laugh when he said, "If your mother wants a party so badly, let her spring for it."

We spent every available moment in each other's company. I realized I'd only had lunch a few times with Morgan since Keith and I married. She'd been upset we eloped, but caved under my exuberance. I was happy, and damn it all, I wanted her to be happy for me. She finally agreed to come around with her corporate attorney for a double date next week.

Meanwhile, my little mind churned with what I had planned for Keith's birthday. I knew exactly what to get him. Grandpa Wallace would turn over in his grave, but I couldn't resist. I felt like a Cheshire cat.

Oh, okay. I'll tell: I bought Keith a Porsche.

He'd mentioned a hundred times how much he loved that car. I did my homework. I investigated the difference between leasing and buying. This is what I learned.

Leasing vs. Owning a Car:

The decision to lease versus buying a car should be based on the financial attractiveness of the lease compared to borrowing the funds to buy the same car. Like most things that involve dollars, it's all about the math.

With a lease, ownership of the car stays with the leasing company. You would lease the car, and be able to use it, for a specific amount of time. Of course, you would also be responsible for repairs (make sure it's under warranty) and any damages. Financially, the size of a lease payment results from the interest rate of the lease and principal to be repaid over the lease term.

Evaluating the attractiveness of a lease is much more than a simple assessment of the payment. Leases vary dramatically in their assumptions, conditions and buyout privileges, which determine economic benefits at the end of the lease term.

The major legal and financial difference between leasing and buying is the ownership of the car. With a purchase, the ownership remains with purchaser. With a lease, the leasing company owns the car.

For each particular situation, you should consult with your accountant to check the tax implications, and be sure to do the math of lease v. ownership. Keep various factors in mind when deciding: miles driven per year, is the car tax deductible, do you change cars frequently?

Since neither Keith nor I had our own business, we couldn't write off the lease through our expenses. And, since the money from Grandpa Wallace's estate was available, I paid cash for the car.

The car dealer practically rubbed his hands together with glee. So, of course, he embellished my options for the car, should I choose to add them. I have to admit this was the most beautiful car I had even seen. Keith would look hot in the driver's seat. I imagined watching his hands on the steering wheel, insisting he find some secluded, sylvan spot, so we could see just how awkward and sexy it would be to make love in the car.

So, here's what I ended up buying:

Carrera S Cabriolet (means convertible)　　*Sticker price $100,635*
Arctic Silver Metallic

Basic Package	*$91,400*
Silver	*825*
Black Interior	*3,365*
Power Seat	*1,550*
19" wheels	*3,900*
Bose High End Sound Package	*1,390*

Destination Charge   *795*
(Shipping from Germany)

MPG: City 18   Highway 26

I planned to frame the window sticker.

The Dealer offered to finance the car through Porsche Financial Services which will set up payments (direct pay program), but I declined, feeling ever so haughty when I said, "I'll pay cash."

Even though, the sales person says the car will go down in value—depreciation of $10,000 per year and $10,000 for each 10,000 miles put on the car, I didn't care. Keith had talked about the car so often and he was sure it would hold its value.

On Saturday morning, the golden moment arrived and I woke Keith up with kisses. He grabbed for me, trying to haul me back into bed but I resisted.

"Come on. Get up, birthday boy. I want to give you your present!"

I stood there, dangling a blindfold from my hand. He grinned and my stomach flip-flopped. I just loved when he looked at me that way.

"What are you going to do?" He wiggled his eyebrows suggestively.

"I'm going to blindfold you. Would you like to dress or go outside naked?"

He tugged on a pair of jeans with no boxers. Oh, baby. I'd keep that visual for a long time. He threw on a sweatshirt, and I tied the blindfold.

I teased him in the elevator, pressing myself against him, whispering how he was going to love me forever when he saw his birthday present. I like watching what my body did to his. Keith had to be the most fun a girl ever had.

The doorman was ready for us. He opened the front door as we passed outside. Once through the doors, I whipped off the blindfold. Keith blinked a couple of times then reacted just as I hoped.

He screamed!

The Porsche sat at the curb, gleaming. A huge red ribbon with an enormous "Happy Birthday" banner draped on the hood. The Porsche salesman had been so excited about the gift that he circled around Keith snapping pictures with his camera. Keith jumped into the car, started it up and laughed like a kid. He left the car running, came out, twirled me around until I was dizzy and kissed me soundly on the lips.

We decided to take a road trip to Connecticut for the weekend.

Our weekend in the Connecticut countryside melted into the work week. I decided to surprise Keith for lunch and stole an extra half hour for the cross-town trek to Goldman Sachs. For whatever foolish reason, this was the first time I ever came to Keith's office. Come to think of it, he'd always come to mine. I had been so caught up in my new job that I hadn't noticed. I made a mental note to be more attentive to his work in the future.

The receptionist directed me down the hall and to the right. I anticipated the look of delight he'd have when he saw me. As I turned the corner, my steps faltered. The only doors before me were swinging double doors that said, "Mail Room."

I plowed through the doors. I didn't have to go any further. I couldn't believe my eyes. The room, complete with mail cubbies, copy and fax machines was empty, but there stood this tiny desk with a name plate on it: Keith Cunningham.

My husband was the mail clerk.

Keith lied to me!

Why did he lead me to believe he was an investment banker? *Suddenly, his demand to keep his own bank account didn't seem so innocent. We had opened a joint account for my inheritance. He'd said his salary was directly deposited and it would stay less complicated if he just wrote me checks as we needed them. Like a fool, I had never questioned his logic.*

My heart pounded. I started twisting the little gold band on my finger. There had to be an answer. My mind started screaming Keith was the conniving scum Morgan first predicted ... then my brain went numb.

Keith, the love of my life could not be a fraud.

Then the door swung open. The room seemed to shrink when Keith entered. Dressed in the navy slacks, white shirt and blue tie I knotted on him just this morning, I thought I'd choke. He looked sexy as hell, even holding a huge grey mail bin. His jaw dropped open.

"Sam! What are you doing here?"

My hand trembled as I pointed to his name plate. "Are you the mail clerk?"

Anger flashed in his eyes. He shrugged as if there was no problem as he slid the bin onto the counter.

"Someone's gotta do it."

"There's nothing wrong with being a mail clerk, Keith. It's just when someone pretends they're someone they're not, a girl starts to wonder what else isn't true." My knees quaked as my world started to crumble. "You told me you were in investments."

He shook his head and tapped me on the nose. Except for a glistening of perspiration breaking on his brow, he was cool as a python.

"I did not. I told you I landed a job at Goldman Sachs. You assumed the rest."

Our old conversations tumbled through my mind. Because I didn't want to appear stupid, I had assigned "distributions" with another meaning.

Damn.

I said, "What did you expect me to think distributions were?"

He pointed to the mail cart. "Well what to you call delivering mail?"

Tears brimmed in my eyes. "Why didn't you tell me?"

He closed his eyes as if to be patient with me. "I couldn't stay unemployed, Sam. I took this until something better would come along."

"That doesn't answer my question." I crossed my arms, tapping my foot.

He dropped his arms in exasperation. "I didn't tell you for the exact reason you're reacting now. Come on! You have a great job, making great money. You inherited all that cash from your Grandpa. Would you have married me if you knew I worked in the mail room?"

I was totally flustered. "Well, of course I would. Who do you think I am?"

Hmm. Did I just lie? I'd have to think about that later.

Frowning, he stood away from me as if I was a stranger. His voice actually trembled. "I thought if you knew, you'd dump me."

I began to back-peddle. "Keith, we're married! I thought we shared everything."

Despair filled his beautiful, brown eyes. "Well, none of this matters anyway. I just took a new job in Connecticut. It not only pays better, but it makes the most of my skills and education."

The bottom dropped out of my reasoning. "You took a job … where?"

"You heard me. It's the opportunity of a lifetime."

"Doing what?"

"Advertising. What I always wanted to do." He grabbed me by the arms, a bit gruffly. "Don't nix this, Sammy. I really busted my butt to get the job. You'll see. I'll be rolling in cash soon, too."

My voice grew soft. "Connecticut is a long commute."

He grinned. "Yeah, but I have a fast, new car. I won't mind a bit."

17

Well, bottom line is, Keith's new job was the end of our marriage. You'd think that discovering his deception would have had me scrambling to get his name off my checking account and protect my assets.

But, no.

I bought his story hook, line and sinker. Keith, my boutique husband, was every girl's dream of a hunk with a heart. I was willing to believe his every word. I swallowed the notion that he hid his occupation for fear that I would find him inferior. My sexy, muscled husband with the silly grin, hungry eyes and magic hands seemed all the more vulnerable. I just worked harder to prove I loved him.

What a sucker I was.

Keith drove to Connecticut every day. Pretty soon, he took an apartment there. The next thing I knew, he demanded a divorce. Keith met someone else in Connecticut.

And we were just about to celebrate our first wedding anniversary.

Stunned into immobility, I let him go. It wasn't until that Monday when our bank statement came, that the enormity of his scandal hit. Keith had emptied our joint bank account.

The son of a bitch stole the rest of my inheritance.

I vomited everything I ate for two weeks.

Morgan vented her outrage by taking my divorce case—which proved an exercise in frustration.

Keith had only paid rent from his account once, the rest of the rent and all the other expenses were paid from our joint account. I was so angry that I had been blind to him using my money. I wanted the Porsche returned. At least I could sell the car and get some cash back.

Morgan shook her head after reading the information. *"Damn it, Sam, you can't even get the car back. The way the law is written, the inheritance was yours. But you gave part of it—the Porsche—away. You titled the car to Keith, and now he owns it. Your gift of the Porsche to your husband was just that: a completed gift. Keith does not have to return it."*

Morgan looked like she wanted to scream. "Those stupid pictures the Porsche dealer took of the car draped in ribbons and the birthday banner sealed your fate. Keith has the title and the proof you gave the car as a gift."

Tears burned a trail down my cheeks. What a fool I'd been. I hated him!

Morgan looked mournful. "Consider yourself lucky, honey. It could have been worse."

I blew my nose. "How is that possible?"

She snorted most unladylike. "How? Listen up, Sam. Keith is no slacker in the fleecing department."

She rounded her shoulders as if bracing for a fight. *"Since you were the breadwinner in the marriage, Keith tried to hit you for alimony. Only because you gave him such a substantial portion of your inheritance, the judge determined that you don't have to pay."*

My blood ran cold. *"He tried to get alimony?"*

Morgan nodded. "Oh, yes. He's a clever little pig."

I shook my head to dispel the confusion. "But, why are you saying I was the breadwinner? He has a job in Connecticut."

Morgan's brows lifted in surprise. "Keith never had a job in Connecticut, Sam. He drove there every day to meet up with his new, rich girlfriend. He was using your money to woo her. I'm sure he tried for alimony to keep up his cash flow. No doubt he'll try marrying this next girl the first chance he gets!"

I sat stunned. I struggled to inhale, thinking I would faint.

Morgan wasn't finished. *"You'll be glad to know, that the judge also ruled in your favor regarding your IRA and 401(k) retirement accounts. Keith tried to take part of them since he helped you make your investment decisions while you supported him."*

I bolted to my feet. *"Hey! I didn't make any investments with him. He had me cash most of it out!"*

Morgan lifted a tailored shoulder. If she considered me a complete idiot, at least she had the good grace not to show it.

"Well the slime bucket sought to attach those funds too. The judge told him, no."

The ice in Morgan's eyes made me flinch as she continued. *"Keith spent one year with you, lived virtually rent and expense free, snagged himself an expensive car and cleaned out the rest of your inheritance."*

My stomach burned as she ticked off those facts. My heart sank as the truth bore into my mind. He never loved me. I had been conned. Deceived, emotionally betrayed, and robbed.

Morgan leaned toward me, tapping a red-nailed finger on her desk, ensuring her information found its mark.

"The bastard lived as if he had a $250,000 salary for a year. Not bad for a scam artist." Her eyes gleamed dangerously. "I'd like to roast his tender parts over open coals."

I paced, swallowing the lava rising in my throat. I thought I might puke all over Morgan's mahogany desk.

My voice broke. "I believed he loved me."

Merciless, Morgan forged on. "Keith demands his name back, too."

My voice turned to venom. "He can have his goddamn name. Why would I want it?"

Lifting a perfect brow, Morgan's words softened. "Do you now understand what a barracuda looks like?"

That did it. My insides erupted. Blinded by tears, I dashed for the ladies room, hoping to vomit the last of Keith Cunningham out of my life forever.

18

W ell, I'd done it. I hit rock bottom. I had squandered all but
fifteen percent of Grandpa Wallace's life savings on a man
with a hot body, nice smile and a smooth tongue. He'd talked circles
around me, kissed me senseless and robbed me blind. He stripped me
of pride, dignity and dollars. Oh, and did I mention, my mother's
confidence?

But, staring at myself in the mirror I had to accept the fact that I
freely gave it all away. I surrendered control of my life to please a man
who loved me on false pretenses. Even if the love had been genuine,
what gave me the license to stop thinking clearly? I had for the last
time naïvely followed my emotions over good financial sense. Even
when my instincts told me Keith was wrong, I let him invade our
nest egg … er, MY nest egg.

I kissed off men for good.

I wouldn't feel this way forever, but for now, it suited me just
fine.

And my budget? Ha! I became the budget queen. If I didn't own
it, I didn't want it. I had plenty of clothes. My apartment suited me
just fine. Eighteen months into my new job and I still congratulated
myself. Not only did the work fascinate me but the pay was excellent,
especially with no one tapping it but me.

What more did I need?

My sole focus became replacing my lost inheritance as quickly as possible.

Because it cost nothing, I took up jogging to keep my mind clear, reflect on my goals and help myself heal. Keith really took a chunk out of me. Running released endorphins that soothed my aching heart and angry thoughts. I couldn't help but wonder who Keith's next victim was. I thought to warn her, but realized I hadn't heeded my own warnings. A barracuda like Keith could dodge any lampoon.

I decided life was good. I drew immense satisfaction from that simple fact. I even saw Parker and Morgan through new eyes. I understood the value of the independence they chose to achieve their goals.

I was four years older but felt like I was just beginning to bloom.

I began traveling often with work. Even hit Paris a few times. Landing in strange airports, staying in hotels alone, meeting and impressing clients helped me discover the real Samantha Davis.

Every month, I gave myself $100 for a travel fund. Montana was calling.

And sometimes I'd think of Alan, and wonder how much more he'd appreciate me now. Then I'd smile. Even that disaster of a relationship had given me some direction. If Alan had accepted me half-formed as I was, would I ever have become the woman I am today?

A little over a year after my divorce, I came home from a business trip to find a flyer under my door. My apartment building planned to convert to condominiums. Residents were being offered the first option to buy them. My studio (or lovingly, the Hallway) was available for $229,000. I decided to run the numbers to see if it made sense to purchase. Grandpa Wallace always said real estate could be a good investment. Buying my condo could help diversify my investment portfolio. I had $10,000 that I could take penalty free from my retirement account and a smidgeon over $25,800 cash that I had saved, so making the move to buy would take consideration. The Hallway also needed to be renovated and that could be expensive.

My heart pumped with excitement as if someone just offered me a puppy. All my neighbors were talking about the condo conversion. I did some homework. Not wanting to bother a realtor if I didn't truly plan to buy elsewhere, I scoured the real estate classifieds. I dropped in at "open houses" for condos, and really focused on ones the same size as mine. Prospective buyers were always welcome to open houses without obligation. I checked the papers to learn the asking prices for condos in my area. *I found that my Hallway was underpriced at $229,000 or would cost, as the realtors said, $325 per square foot.* But, my place needed updating.

Another consideration was that my condo was tiny. I didn't want to live here for the rest of my life. However, the condo conversion documents said that as an owner, I could rent the property. That was excellent news. I would have choices in the future. Should I choose to move out in a year or two, I could either sell and use the cash to upgrade to a larger home; or purchase another property and rent the Hallway. This was an excellent move for my investment portfolio.

Seemed like a win-win situation to me. It would take all of my savings and part of my retirement account (IRA/401(k)), but I believed this would be a wise decision. Mom agreed. So did Morgan. That meant something! But, her blessing didn't come easily. Of course, she gave me the drill:

"Now, Sam, the best way to decide if buying your condo is a good investment is to consider the property itself. Its size, location and future value. Do you think your apartment will increase in value?"

I blinked a couple of times.

Stifling a grin, Morgan held up a stopping hand. "Think about this. *You'll be taking on $229,000 of debt. Whether the value or your property increases or decreases, you'll be responsible for that amount."*

I said, *"From the conversations I had with realtors at the open houses, the market has been climbing steadily over the past years."*

"What about 'real estate bubbles'?"

"Do they sell those?"

Morgan laughed. "No, silly. *Those are times when the real estate market flattens. Prices drop or just level off like in 2008. Would you be confident buying your place at that price should the market drop?*"

Slowly, I nodded. "It's Upper East Side. The location will always attract renters or buyers. No matter what, I could make my payments, and the neighborhood wasn't hit too hard during the real estate bubble."

She clapped her hands. "Good! LOCATION, LOCATION, LOCATION! That makes your investment worthwhile. Go buy yourself a condo. This is wonderful."

Now, I needed a mortgage.

I headed off to my bank to see what they could teach me. My account manager was quick to answer my questions. What really got to me were the different options. Hold on to your chardonnay. Here goes:

TYPES OF MORTGAGES:

1. *FIXED RATE MORTGAGE. Typically, based on PRIME (which is the Fed Funds target rate plus three) and can extend for 15 or 30 years. It is 'fixed' because it has a 'fixed' payment. Usually, the monthly payments for a 15 year mortgage will be higher than the 30 year monthly payments. Both will charge part interest and part principal. (Principal is the amount borrowed.) Remember: do the math for the entire term of the mortgage to see what you're really going to pay.* **TIP:** *Nowadays, there's a wonderful opportunity called bi-monthly payments. You can take advantage of the lower 30 year interest rate, but set up with the lending bank to pay half the monthly payment twice a month. (Instead of paying, say $2000 on the 1st of the month, you pay $1000 on the 1st, and $1000 on the 15th. Half to principal, half to interest.) This reduces your loan amount significantly enough that a 30 year mortgage is paid off in about 18 years. You pay a fee for this service, but it's worth the savings in interest payments.*

2. *ADJUSTABLE RATE MORTGAGE (ARM). The rate on this mortgage adjusts depending on the marketplace for the underlying*

rate vehicle. In other words, the mortgage rate adjusts according to the current rate of vehicles such as PRIME and LIBOR. (Sometimes called, English or London LIBOR). PRIME as noted in #1 is based on the rates the US Federal Reserve sets. LIBOR stands for the London Inter-Bank Offered Rate and is a widely used benchmark for short term interest rates. LIBOR is the rate of interest at which banks borrow funds from other banks in the London inter-bank market. So, it is similar to our Federal Funds rate (see Appendix B). **TIP:** Always check LIBOR, because many times it is the better rate. You'll probably have to go to a brokerage/investment house for this. I would recommend you either check the websites or just walk in the door and ask.

3. *BALLOON v. INTEREST-ONLY. These two terms have to do with the amount of principal paid, and when it is paid. A balloon loan has a substantial amount of the principal due at some point in the loan, usually 10 years. (In my case, it would be about $100,000). Interest-only will usually mean you pay only interest for an amount of time, usually 10 years, and after that, your monthly payments will substantially increase to cover the principle.* Again, whatever works best for you. You can only determine that by doing the math!

NOTE: Mortgage Insurance is usually required by lenders if a buyer puts less than 20% of the purchase price down as deposit. Mortgage insurance can be very expensive ($80 per month for the life of the loan. In Sam's case $28,800!) Most companies, however, will waive the insurance after a certain number of years of consistent mortgage payments, or 20% equity in the property is reached. Still, the buyer must request the mortgage insurance be removed after the grace period. The lender won't remove the fee unless requested!

Example for an Adjustable Rate/Interest Only Loan*: You may take a 30 year loan on your property. Ten (10) year interest-only based on six (6) month LIBOR. After ten years, you would begin to pay off the principal. However, there are no prepayment penalties. So, should you choose, you can pay down the principal (the loan amount) along with the* *interest as you go along. As an adjustable loan, the rate will change every six (6) months and could be as little as 1 5/8 percent over six (6) month LIBOR (which trades like the U.S. government security six (6) month bill).* In other words—Cheap! Cheap! Cheap!) Keep in mind that interest rates can go up and down with this type of loan. Payments change every six months. So, some months could be laughingly low, others may pinch a bit. And when interest rates go up, your payment could go up—fast! Be careful!

I decided to really challenge my finance acumen. No typical, consistent home mortgage for me. I chose a home loan from a mortgage company* that specialized in LIBOR based home loans. (LIBOR, again, is the London Inter-Bank Offering Rate. So I would use an international based rate to pay my U.S. mortgage. Other mortgage companies base their rates on PRIME which is set by the Federal Government.)

Thanks to Mom for making up the difference, I was able to put down a 20% deposit to avoid paying mortgage insurance. Before leaving for work, I sat at the counter gazing at my new mortgage sheet. This is how the numbers broke down for my monthly payments:

Purchase Amount:	*$229,000.00*
Less Down-payment:	*-$ 45,000.00*
TOTAL MORTGAGE:	*$183,200.00*
6 month LIBOR plus 1 5/8 = 4.50%	*$ 8,224.00*
Taxes and Insurance	*$ 5,380.00*
Condo Fee	*$ 5,400.00*
TOTAL EXPENSES	*$ 19,024.00*
TOTAL MONTHLY PAYMENT	*$ 1,585.00*

Wow! By purchasing my condo, my payment was over $500 less a month than rent! With that kind of savings, I could budget for a new kitchen and maybe a marble bathroom. Oooh, and I could modernize the closets! Shoe shopping and spa treatments faded in their allure compared to this great investment. My fingers itched to begin the Hallway's make-over. Living with some construction mess would be well worth increasing the value of my property.

I laced up my Nikes and headed out for a jog, my veins humming with the warmth of financial satisfaction. With a little piece of Manhattan to call my own, my purchase strategy laid out and my lost inheritance slowly on the mend, I felt as if I walked ten feet above the planet. Fixed rate mortgages. ARMs. LIBOR. Taxes, Titles and Insurance. I understood it all. Who needed chocolate when Finance gave the same rush? I was hooked. No turning back. I had become a finance addict.

19

I greeted familiar faces on my morning jog. I had joined a group training for the Susan G. Komen Race for the Cure. Knowing that I was running to help cure breast cancer boosted my self-esteem. I had sound health, and was running to help raise awareness and money for those with this terrible disease. It felt great to wave to fellow joggers with the same goals.

I slowed my pace, too enamored with the morning to race through it, and padded deeper into the park, feeling the weight of my ponytail bounce between my shoulders.

A biker came over the rise, pedaling fast. He looked like any biker with the slanted sun glasses and helmet, but I couldn't help to notice how magnificent his lean body looked in his riding gear.

My mind warned, Oh, no, Stella. No men. Not yet.

So, like any lady, I just smiled, focused on the path and jogged on.

When I heard the brakes squeal, I didn't give it another thought. I didn't even hear him ride up beside me.

"Samantha, is that you?"

Oh God. I knew that voice in my sleep. My heart stopped, but my feet just couldn't. My eyes shot to his face. I had to stop. My knees already started to buckle.

Okay, be cool, I told myself. You can do this.

"Alan?"

He stopped his bike inches from me. "Sam, I can't believe it's you."

He pulled off his sunglasses. When had his eyes gotten so blue? I wanted to say something, but my throat tightened. I had a sudden desire to bop him in the nose for leaving me on that sidewalk all those years ago. But, that was the old, un-addicted Sam. Me? I possessed power now.

His eyes raked me from head to toe. He smiled. "It's been a long time."

I managed to keep my face cordial. "Yes, indeed."

"How are you?"

A bubble of laughter escaped. "Better than ever, I must say."

He nodded slowly, his eyes light with mischief. "I can see that."

I guess he could. Spandex jogging outfits left little for the imagination. His gaze tore over me as if he was starving.

I wiped my sweaty palms on my thighs. Alan had a way of making my pulse race.

Guess I had to ask. "And, how are you?"

He was silent a moment, watching me.

I felt myself frown. "You okay?"

He shrugged. "I always wanted to apologize for treating you like a jerk. Now here you are and I'm tongue-tied."

Oh, I could do this. I nodded in agreement. "Yes, you were a jerk."

He winced. "I deserve that."

I let my gaze slide from his face to the field behind him.

He inched forward to intercept my vision. "Given up on men?"

I delivered the barb smooth as silk. "They haven't proven too reliable."

"Ouch."

I waved away his discomfort. "I've been on a personal quest."

"Oh, yeah? Has it been productive?"

I laughed. Typical Alan. "Actually, yes. I've done pretty well for myself."

To my surprise, he beamed.

"I can see it in your face. Somehow, you've changed."

He touched my cheek with the tip of his finger, as if daring to make physical contact. "I've never seen you look more beautiful."

"Now, stop, Alan." I took his hand in mine in a gesture of friendship. "It really is good to see you again. I've got to finish my run now."

The way my heart pounded, I could outrace Amtrak. I turned to go.

"I'm not dating anyone, either." He pedaled his bike slowly beside me.

Damn the raised brow. I couldn't help it. "Oh, yes?"

He grabbed my arm, bringing us both to a halt. "If you would give me the chance, I'd love to apologize properly."

I huffed a long breath. "Okay, shoot."

He looked around. "Not here. Can I take you to dinner?"

I didn't have plans on the horizon. I didn't mind before, but now my lack of social life seemed lame.

I shook my head. "I've been really busy."

He sighed. "How about next week."

I crumbled. "Are you plotting to break my heart again?"

He looked truly dumbfounded. "I broke your heart?"

I shrugged. "Guess I put more into our relationship than you did." I held up a stopping hand. "It's okay, though. I've come a long way since then."

He actually swallowed hard. "Sam, I had a lot of static that you didn't know about while we dated. I took my stress out on you. I am truly sorry."

My arms fell at my side in surrender. "Alright, if you insist on hashing this out, we can go out Wednesday night."

His laugh resounded with relief. "Nothing would please me more."

He bit his lower lip as if fighting a question.

I couldn't resist. "What?"

"Do you still have that blue dress?"

My Stella McCartney? With my budget? Of course. I nodded slowly. "Yes."

Warmth filled his eyes. "I've often thought about it."

My gut twisted with memories of him watching me in that dress. I pushed the thought away.

"Oh no, Mr. Abercrombie, we are not picking up where we left off."

He just grinned. "Do you live at the same place?"

I hesitated before giving his shoulder a little poke. "I own it now."

Admiration lit his eyes. "Great investment."

I chuckled. "You haven't changed a bit. What time should I expect you?"

"Seven." He hid those gorgeous eyes behind his shades again, started to roll away, then stopped. "Are you still always late? I just need to know so I can time it better."

"I'll see you at seven," I said, unable to stop the grin creasing my lips.

He waved good bye and I waited until he was out of sight before I collapsed onto the grass. Heaven help me. I accepted a date with Alan Abercrombie. My first love. My first broken heart. The first reason why I should have said, no!

Holy smokes.

I'd broken my one year fast.

Even though I had four days until our date, I resisted ripping through my closet to find the perfect dress. The old Samantha would have done that. No, wait. The old Samantha would have flown to Bloomie's for a new outfit. Instead, I stripped to shower, thinking about the renovations for the Hallway.

Once the kitchen and bath were finished, I'd start entertaining again. Gutted now, the kitchen was unusable at the moment. *I budgeted $10,000 to do both kitchen and bath. I'd learned from Morgan that any improvements to my property can be added to the cost basis (purchase price plus improvements, check www.irs.gov for today's* *rules) of the condo should I decide to sell, and would reduce my capital gain exposure. So, I got three estimates for the jobs, chose the lowest one (it was the cutest guy too), and have all my renovation receipts in a file. Now, I can make $250,000 tax free (providing the condo increases in value that much), and with any luck at all, when I sell, the profit will exceed that amount and I can add all the renovation costs to the cost basis. Not only would I recoup my investment, but earn a nice profit for living in saw-dust and a renovated apartment. I'll have basically "lived for free" if all goes according to plan.*

Living for free. What a fantastic concept. It's not easy to pull off, but do-able if I'm smart about it. So, I'll only remodel parts of the condo that will increase the value of the property, like the kitchen and bathroom first, and not buy new furniture until I can afford it.

In the meantime, I could buy some candles, cushy pillows, fun dishes and chopsticks and serve dinner around the coffee table oriental style.

I turned my face into the cold shower to quell thoughts of entertaining Alan one-on-one around the coffee table. Brrrrr. The thought of commitment sent a shiver through me. I turned the shower to hot. I needed to loosen up those muscles bunching my neck. I'd call Morgan as soon as I finished showering. She'd ensure I keep my head on straight.

On Wednesday evening, the doorman, Dave, with whom I have become great friends, buzzed at exactly seven announcing Alan's arrival. I took one last look in the mirror. Chandelier earring peeked through my hair doing the gypsy thing. I put a little 'sugar plum' lip gloss on, then sashayed from the Hallway telling myself the strapless, slinky black number with my shoulders smoothed and glowing bare were only an after- thought. I felt control right down to my pedicure.

Both Alan and Dave reacted on cue.

"Close your mouth, Dave," Alan said, grinning back at me.

I laughed. "Where are we headed?"

One glance at Alan and I was in danger. His navy suit, white shirt and Hermes tie seemed to hug him like a woman in love. The unabashed enjoyment in his eyes as he gazed at me set off all sorts of alarms like, Fire! Take the nearest Exit! Combustion in ten seconds!

Alan offered me his arm.

I took it, letting a bubble of laughter tickle its way up my throat and out into open air.

Dave held the door open for us.

"See ya, Dave," Alan said. Leaning toward me he whispered, "You smell great."

"Nice to see you two together again!" Dave winked at me.

I waved absently to Dave, my eyes riveted on Alan's face as he led me to a waiting Towncar. I suddenly felt this moment had been way too long in coming. If only I'd known. I would have wrestled a fire extinguisher into my purse.

Alan slid in next to me, grinning. "Do you still like Japanese food?"

"Oh, yeah."

"Good. I found a place you're going to love."

The limo was already pulling away from the curb. My heart pounded with the steady rhythm of pure pleasure. We smiled at each other like two kids with a secret. I wasn't the least surprised when he kissed my knuckles as if thanking me for accepting the date.

"I thought about you for years, Sam."

I pursed my lips, to keep from smiling. "Are you still at Credit Suisse?"

He nodded. "I'm head of the desk, now. I get to dish the dirt instead of eating it." Those blue eyes held mine captive. "And you? Still with the law firm?"

"No. I've been with a technology company for almost two years now. I love it. Lots of travel." I grinned. "I've been to Paris twice."

He slapped a hand over his heart. "I've always wanted to see Paris. We'll have to go."

I gave him a wary look. "Maybe."

He must have taken my caution as his cue. He shook his head. "I was such an idiot when we dated, Samantha. I don't blame you for being cautious, now."

I laid a hand on his arm, just for old times. "The words bimbo and bubble brain propelled me to higher ground, Alan. You were cruel, but you spoke the truth."

He scrubbed his face with his hand, embarrassment clear. "What a moron I was."

I shrugged my bare shoulder. "Well, something good came from our dating fiasco. I learned the difference between a stock and a bond. You can quiz me anytime."

A grateful smile tugged at his lips. "You're amazing, Sam."

I laughed. "You ain't seen nothing yet, honey."

Alan reached for a bottle of champagne chilling in a silver bucket. I had been so preoccupied with him that I hadn't noticed it. He expertly popped the cork and we both grinned. When we each had a crystal flute in our hands he tapped his glass to mine.

"I get the impression you've been ground through the mill."

Laughter escaped my lips before I could stop it. "Let's just say the old bimbo took a few more hits before she earned her Ph.D. in deadbeat lovers."

He whistled softly. "That's harsh."

I shook my head. "You have no idea, Alan. I was actually married for a year to a man who fleeced me out of my grandfather's inheritance and every penny in my bank account." I briefly closed my eyes, angry with myself for blurting out this embarrassing truth. I met his gaze, surprised to see concern there.

He looked shocked. "What happened, Sam?"

I held up a stopping hand. "Maybe later, Alan. The story would ruin our evening."

We sat in silence for a while, sipping our champagne until I changed the subject. "So, what have you been doing these past years?"

"Trying to forget you." He said this so softly, that his words hit like a thunder clap.

I stared at him stunned, while my mind furiously commanded me not to believe his sentence. Oh, no. I laughed, and thank the stars, it sounded genuine.

"Oh, that's smooth, Alan."

His brows did this momentary twist of anguish before he grinned. "Well, it's the truth." He gazed out the window now that we'd come to a stop light. "Remember when we were dating and I told you my mother was ill?" He turned his gaze back to me, I'm sure, to gauge my response.

I nodded. "I remember. Is she better?"

He gulped his champagne as if swallowing a large pill. "I guess you could say so. She wasn't really sick."

"What do you mean?"

"My father was divorcing her for his secretary. It caused a huge battle."

I found my fingers flexing over the muscles in his arm. "Why didn't you tell me, Alan?"

He captured my hand. "Because I was too stupid to confide in you."

Excuses. Bad behavior and now, more excuses. I'd bought Keith's excuses once. I did not trust myself to listen to Alan's. Then Alan went and did it. Admitted fault.

He ran a hand through his hair. "I took my anger out on you, Sam. My father's secretary was such a bimbo while my mother was educated and confident. With your naiveté, I pasted my Dad's secretary on your face. I am truly sorry."

I held up a stopping hand. "Don't say another word." I really didn't want to believe him. But then again, if not, why was I here?

Those blue eyes swam with emotion. "There's no one out there like you. You're gorgeous, sincere, smart, funny—the entire package. When I realized that, it was too late."

I chugged the rest of my champagne. My heart was doing this flip-flop thing, my pulse made my hands sweat. I met those bedroom eyes and hoped he read the sincerity in mine.

"What am I supposed to say to that, Alan?"

He chewed his lip as if he'd just made the biggest ass of himself. "Say nothing, Sam. Just give me a chance. I don't care how long it takes."

I liked the sound of that. The ball was in my court. I held out my flute for another hit of champagne. "Well then, I'll toast to starting as friends, Alan. I always loved your jokes."

He laughed, poured more champagne and Whamo, the tension burst and disappeared like one of the bubbles in my glass. We talked about work. He asked about my Mom, Parker and Morgan. He confessed he still summered with his merry band of men. Soon, the limo pulled up before this red door with no sign indicating a restaurant at all.

Alan cocked an eyebrow. "This is Manhattan's best kept secret for sushi. Prepare to die from delight."

I stepped out of the limo, unwilling to admit that I already had.

20

After two months of dating, I finally told Alan about Keith and my financial loss. We were in my Hallway. Alan pulled me into his lap, giving me his full attention while I rehashed the ugly parts. His warmth and support helped solidify the foundation we had slowly begun rebuilding between us. But, there was no mistaking the vengeance in those baby-blues of his. To this day, I wonder what strings he pulled to make Keith's life a nightmare.

Alan also checked my current portfolio and gave it his stamp of approval. He complimented me for the discipline I used in getting myself swiftly out of debt. He actually called me a financial wizard.

Imagine that. Me, the bimbo. I kissed him and corrected him saying that I had actually become a finance addict.

My current portfolio looks like this: One (1) studio condominium with a large Hallway, on the Upper East Side in New York City. The kitchen is currently being renovated, which requires that I do dishes in the bathroom sink. There is saw dust on most of my clothes, but I live alone so the inconvenience is manageable. Hopefully, the renovations will increase the value of this, my most valuable, investment.

401(k) retirement plan with a value of $49,792.00 on the last statement—not bad for six (6) years. The matching programs that both *companies provided really made a difference. Like Morgan told me—free money.*

Five (5) different stocks of 100 shares each which I still have from Grandpa. I am determined to learn how to trade stocks soon.

No, and I mean NO, credit card debt.

And, my favorite, One (1) very handsome boyfriend! Not a bad portfolio for a 29 year old girl from a small town in Pennsylvania.

He laughed. He handed me back my portfolio predicting I'd see more growth in no time. Then, he kissed me, and promised to help paint the new kitchen.

Everything snow-balled from there. Alan and I remained an item when my thirtieth birthday came into view. From where I stood, thirty looked all shiny and wonderful this crisp and cold new year. I couldn't believe I'd reached this landmark. I faced thirty with crystal clear vision and what I had come to realize was a solid, loving relationship between Alan and me. I didn't need his money for security. He didn't need mine. I could speak with him in his own language about business and vice versa. We learned how to make the best of our down time, traveling when we could and staying in when we needed. We lived to make each other happy, and found happiness in our own accomplishments.

I could do thirty. Easy.

Well, it seems Alan thought so, too. I caught him head to head with Parker one rare night at her place. She and Franco had gotten married a year ago. They had a small civil ceremony in New York, and I was Parker's witness. The next day, they jetted off to Italy where they married again in his family's village church and threw a huge reception there. Lucky for me, I was able to work some business around the trip, so I attended the party and wrote the expenses off for the business end of the trip—including the flight.

Anyway, when I caught them head-to-head my suspicions grew. I wedged myself between them at the table.

I said, "Okay, what are you two hatching here?"

Parker rolled her eyes. "See, Alan? I told you it wouldn't work."

Alan grinned. "Well, it'll be easier if she knows anyway."

I felt my eyes light up. "Ooooh! You're planning a birthday party."

Parker laughed. "Alan, we're busted. Sam, you're frustrating, but so damned cute."

I hugged her wanting to know how I could help, who was coming, where the party would be, how many people we could invite, yada, yada, yada.

Alan pulled me onto his lap. "Hold on, now. You can offer suggestions, but this is our party for you."

Parker patted me on the shoulder. "And you've come a long way, baby."

It seemed that everyone was charged up to celebrate the fact that I've been walking this planet for thirty years. I found myself grinning at the stupidest times. Everyone's affection warmed me right down to my toes.

I suddenly realized with 30 on the horizon, I should double-check my 401(k) investments, and readjust to a slightly more conservative approach. It's time to move from an Aggressive Growth portfolio to a Growth portfolio. And, I will have to check into doing a little more international growth, too. Ah! Freedom! It feels so good!

On my birthday, Alan picked me up early and we stopped to grab Parker and Franco. My gaze settled on Alan's profile as the taxi maneuvered through traffic. He smiled at me. Every time his lips twisted into that grin, my pulse raced a tad faster until I could breathe again.

The party room at Savigne was glorious, intimate and crammed with everyone I knew. Dinner was divine—how could it not be with Franco and Parker handling the menu? Before I knew it, the waiters wheeled out this fabulous French confection in two layers with white and dark chocolate shavings covered with strawberries. Thirty candles blazed on the cake. I clapped my hands together, holding them against my chest to keep my heart in check because everyone was singing 'Happy Birthday'. Alan sang the loudest. He stood by the cake, love clear in those blue eyes, singing his heart out with his arms open wide. Tears started to blur my vision. I hastily wiped them away.

I swallowed the knot in my throat as everyone yelled, "Make a wish!"

I closed my eyes, wishing this wonderful moment in my life would last forever. I inhaled what seemed like all the oxygen in the room and slowly blew out each darned candle until a plume of smoke curled up from the cake.

Everyone cheered and Alan swept me into his arms, kissing me soundly on the lips. I heard champagne corks popping all around us. "Happy Birthday, Honey," he whispered against my lips. Man, he tasted good.

I turned to cut the cake.

Alan said, "Wait a minute, Sam."

I looked up expectantly.

He slid a flute of champagne into my hands. All around me everyone held up a glass, their gazes shimmering with expectation. They all knew something that I didn't. Each and every one grinned from ear to ear.

I looked at the crowd. I looked at Alan. "What?"

He stepped closer. "It's my turn to make a toast."

The room had grown quiet.

I sensed mischief in his eyes. "You going to tell everyone all the bad stuff you know about me?"

He laughed. I heard my mother chuckle.

"No." He lightly pinched my chin. "I want to tell everyone how we met seven years ago. How you swept me off my feet just by walking past me on the wharf in Newport. I want to tell them how miserable I was all those years after we broke up. And, how I wondered where you were, what you were doing, and if you ever thought of me. I want to tell them how my world began to turn again that day I found you in Central Park. I want to tell them how my life is so full with you in it. How I jump out of bed in the morning because I know after a day of busting my tail at work, we'll meet afterwards and the sun will shine all over again. I want to tell them how very much I love you, and how very much I want to you to be my wife."

I practically dropped my champagne. My heart thudded.

He got down on one knee. He reached into his pocket and pulled out a black velvet box. The room was so silent I could hear my own breathing as he lifted the lid.

A diamond, pale blue like a robin's egg, like the sky, like my eyes, glittered on a band of pure platinum. My hand flew to my lips. I gasped.

"Samantha."

My eyes riveted on his. My pulse raced. My mouth grew dry. Oh, God, the love reflecting in his eyes! I said, "Yes, Alan?"

"Will you marry me?"

My knees grew weak but I pulled myself into the epitome of grace. I glanced at my mother. I knew what she was thinking: if only Dad and Grandpa Wallace were here. A tear ran down her cheek, but I understood. This time, it was good.

I laid my hand on Alan's shoulder, leaned down, kissed him lightly on the lips, and said, "Yes, Alan Abercrombie. I will marry you!"

Alan slid that incredible ring onto my finger, kissed my hand, and that was all I remembered for the next hour. The place became bedlam. I embraced the love, caring and friendship from every person at my party. And not for a single moment did I take my arm from the future father of my children, because a finance addict knows when her investments are sound - both emotionally and financially. From where I stood, life was so perfect I couldn't wait to see what would happen next.

PART II

21

The morning after our engagement, I laid in bed just staring at my ring, steeped in a giddy stupor. I'm marrying my first and true love!

Fantastic!

But, I started to feel queasy. The ghost of Keith began to haunt me. You see? My thirtieth birthday also brought another landmark. Now, I was a finance junkie. I understood finance far better than I had seven years ago. I had lost an inheritance, an expensive car, and my innocence. I'd switched careers and gained a financially rewarding job, a slowly growing investment portfolio and owned my condo.

Marrying Alan would do two things: First, complete the circle of my personal life, and second, make all that was mine, his. YIKES!

Of course, all that was his would become mine, too, but from watching his parent's messy divorce, even he knew that boundaries needed to be set from the beginning, or both parties could get hurt. Alan had done nothing to remotely raise suspicions of fleecing me, (he has far more money than I) or faking his love. Alan was the real deal, but my emotions twitched anyway. Part of my healing over these past years was to promise myself never to be burned again. While I loved Alan with every fiber of my being, and knew I always would, I wanted legal protection in this marriage.

I wanted a pre-nuptial agreement.

I told Alan this at lunch.

He got quiet, those blue eyes watching passersby out the window, while concentrating elsewhere. Then, he nodded. "Okay. I can understand your fears. But, I'll never give you reason to use it. The pre-nup will turn to dust in our safe."

Any guy willing to say that deserves to marry me!

The next day, I took the familiar hallway down to Morgan's office to learn what I needed for my pre-nuptial agreement. Phone to her ear, Morgan waved me in with a smile, the Manhattan skyline offering a spectacular backdrop through the windows behind her.

I forgot to mention, Morgan became engaged to her corporate attorney. Remember? The guy she insisted would never know what hit him that fateful night I'd met Keith. My friend, the Ice Queen, had finally agreed to tie the knot!

Before I could seat myself, she hung up the phone and came around the desk for a hug. She offered me a seat, her eyes alive with interest. "I'm so glad you've decided to protect your assets, Sam. You never know what the future will bring."

I shook my head. "I know there won't be any need for this, but a pre-nup will give me security. I still get creditor calls about Keith's debts."

"It's not easy to get over having your money stolen, especially by a spouse," Morgan agreed. "A wise, older woman once said, 'Never marry a man you wouldn't want to be divorced from!'"

I rolled my eyes at her corny joke then reached for a pen and pad from my bag.

"Okay, Morgan, teach me what I need to know."

She sat across from me, ready to go. *"Now, first, a pre-nup only protects the here and now. It can only represent existing parties, not non-existing parties such as future children. A pre-nup provides that any assets you own prior to the marriage, such as real estate, stays with you in case of divorce."* She held up a knowing finger. *"And, any unconscionable or illegal clauses could seriously jeopardize the credibility of your pre-nup with a judge."*

"Got it. No coercion." I grinned, loving my savvy friend and her storehouse of knowledge. She beamed with energy.

"Next, a pre-nup cannot be signed under duress. If Alan presented you with a prenuptial agreement prior to walking down the aisle of your pre-planned wedding, a judge would consider the pre-nup null and void. Ample time must be given to allow you to obtain your own representation. You should seek a matrimonial lawyer familiar with the laws in your state."

I thought about Keith in Connecticut free as a bird and running around in the Porsche I bought with my good money. "I incurred so much of Keith's debt. How do I protect myself if Alan goes hog-wild with expenses?"

"Simple. You add a clause protecting both you and your spouse from each other's debts." She sat back, satisfied. "This keeps "I do" from meaning, "I owe."

I laughed. "Oh, you're full of wit with the legal jargon."

She smiled. "You'll keep your condo in your name, right?"

I met her gaze. "Yes."

Morgan nodded, satisfied. "Good. Write that down. You worked hard for that property. Include a clause to protect existing real estate assets and your securities accounts.

"Also, keep in mind there are nine community property states: Arizona, California, Idaho, Louisiana, Nevada, New Mexico, Texas, Washington and Wisconsin. These states maintain that what you owned before the marriage remains yours and everything you gain during the marriage is split. The remaining states are marital property states. Assets are divided according to what the court deems fair."

Oh, yes. Knowing this information sent shivers of power down my spine. I wanted to hear it all. I leaned forward, pen poised. "What else?"

She shrugged. "Of course, both parties must fully disclose their assets."

"Of course."

"Both parties need their own lawyers. Don't use Alan's. Get your own."

I planned to have Morgan represent me. I winked at her. "Okay."

"And, in addition to being completely honest in both your disclosures, don't be afraid to ask for more money than you really want. If your intended has a good attorney, he'll start low. Just remember you always deserve more."

I laughed. "Like negotiating for a job."

She clapped her hands. "Exactly. Then, after all is signed, you review the pre-nup every few years of the marriage to update any new assets brought into the marriage, including children." She wiggled her eyebrows.

"Don't push kids yet, Morgan, unless you want to be pushing a stroller right next to me!"

She waved away my concern. "You and Alan will make beautiful babies."

I grinned. "Yeah. It'll be great."

We sat in amicable silence for a moment. The satisfaction of knowing I was building a financial safety net under my future happiness offered a sense of freedom I hadn't expected. Bless Morgan and her wisdom.

"Thank you," I murmured. "Now, may I enlist your services?"

She tapped her chin with a perfectly burnished fingernail. "Sammy, I'm not going to represent you on this matter."

I blinked in surprise. "Why not? You were such a bull dog burying Keith. I thought for sure you'd champion my pre-nuptial agreement."

She said, "In my opinion, you need to negotiate for a high annual income. I don't want to piss off my best friend's future husband. So, why don't I just recommend someone to handle this one detail?"

I raised a questioning brow. "You think I should get tough?"

She reached for her phone and punched a few numbers. "Not tough. Fair. You should get what a woman running your household should expect. Daniel Evans is the guy for you."

Before I knew it, I had a meeting with my very own attorney. Daniel Evans turned the prenuptial agreement from a sweet, yours and mine document to an uncompromising demand on protecting my present and future assets.

Since I am sure that my love for Alan will last a lifetime, I felt the demands seemed a tad, shall we say, aggressive. But, Mr. Evans insisted I enjoy the satisfaction of guarding my material assets, should some unforeseen disaster or mid-life crisis ruin our marriage. As he said, with a shrug, "No one has a crystal ball for the future."

I could hardly argue the point, especially remembering how easily and legally Keith had stolen everything from me.

I looked Daniel Evans straight in the eye. "Why don't you just shoot that document over to Alan's attorney?"

That night at my apartment, I expected Alan to be miffed at my prenuptial demands, so I dressed provocatively to distract him, just in case. I poured myself into my favorite Nicole Miller jeans and peach silk and lace top. I used just a touch of my favorite Gucci perfume in all the right spots and curled my hair. I slid into a pair of B. Brian Atwood's, knowing those five inches still kept me shorter than Alan, Mmmm.

My effort had the desired effect. After plastering me against the wall with his body and covering my neck with kisses, we made our way to my tiny kitchen where he lifted me onto the granite countertop and let his hands linger against my hips. You should know the heat those palms possess. He held me firmly in place with a stupid grin on his face, and said, "Why don't we just get through this pre-nup business so we can enjoy a steamy, romantic dinner."

I can never resist touching him, and gently pushed a stray, blond lock off his forehead. I asked, "Are you angry?"

He pulled the prenuptial agreement from his back pocket, rolled it, and tucked it into the deep-V of my Victoria's Secret neckline.

"Here. Signed. Sealed. Delivered."

I was dumbfounded. I took the document out of my top and looked at it. "What? No questions? No arguments?" I looked down at myself. "I even dressed for battle."

He shook his head, his eyes bright with amusement. In between kisses, he said, "No, my little finance addict. I'm proud of you for protecting yourself. (Kiss on my cheek.) You can have your $30,000 each year. (Kiss on my other cheek.) You can have your Hallway. (Kiss. Kiss on my neck.) I hope you make tons of money with it in the future. (Lower kiss.) Half of all of mine will always be yours." (Even lower kiss.)

I melted like a lip gloss in one hundred degree heat.

Pulling back, he nodded his approval. "Hell. You can have it all! I'm so in love with you, girl. You could have asked for the moon, and I would have delivered it in ribbons. Then he grasped my upper arms, doing great things to my cleavage. You're mine, honey. You were very clever in negotiating this prenuptial. Now, I know you'll be like a lioness protecting me and our kids."

Tears filled my eyes. Something like a whispered, "Oh," fell from my lips.

His grin practically made my Nicole Miller jeans smoke on their own. He said, "And Honey? Dress for battle every day, okay? I like it."

22

The pressure of our wedding was breathing down our necks, so we accepted my mother's invitation to join her for the weekend in the Berkshires. The pile of receipts, magazines, menus, photos and bills commanding the center of the table seemed less daunting in such a peaceful spot. I'll always remember watching Alan and my mother talking head to head as they discussed our wedding budget.

Alan and I had made initial deposits at the Waldorf Astoria for our reception. Parker and her husband, Franco, whose restaurant now thrived in Soho, promised to work with the Waldorf to ensure everything was perfect. So, I had no worries there. One by one, Alan lifted the deposit receipts for the DJ, the florist, for my dress (I loved it!), the photographer, and the limos to compare with his notes. We were on budget and feeling fine.

Alan seemed satisfied. He said, *"My father mentioned he's going to give us a $26,000 gift as a wedding present."*

"Wow! That's nice of him!"

I blew him a kiss from across the table. He smiled and swung an arm around my Mom's shoulder. "I'm paying for the rehearsal dinner. Your Mom's insisting on paying for the reception."

I looked at Mom incredulously. "No, Mom. I'll pay."

My mother winked. "I want to do this. And besides, it's my honor as your Mother to pay. I only wish your Father was here to walk you down the aisle. He would be so proud.

"Alan's Father and I have discussed gifting you both the maximum amount the IRS allows us to give without having to pay taxes. We love you two so much and want you to have some extra cash to start your lives together."

I was overwhelmed by our parents' generosity. I quickly learned that when it comes to gifting the news is very good! The IRS allows you to accept all the gifts anyone is willing to give you. Imagine that! *As the Giftee (you), you are under no obligation legally to mention gifts. The Giftor (your parents, most probably), is only permitted to gift $13,000 annually to each of you. Alan's father planned to give $13,000 to Alan and $13,000 to me. Any amount above $13,000, and the Giftor is required to pay a gift tax.*

Here's the IRS Tax Tip for Gifting:

If you gave any one person gifts valued at more than $13,000, you must report the total gifts to the Internal Revenue Service and may have to pay tax on the gifts (for 2013 and later—check to see if the rules have changed at www.irs.gov). The person who receives your gift does not have to report the gift to the IRS or pay gift or income tax on its value. Gifts include money and property, including the use of property without expecting to receive something of equal value in return. If you sell something at less than its value or make an interest-free or reduced-interest loan, you may be making a gift.

There are some exceptions to the tax rules on gifts. The following gifts do not count against the annual limit:
• *Tuition or Medical Expenses that you pay directly to an educational or medical institution for someone's benefit. (We'll get into tuition and medical expenses later. It's important that you understand this information first ... before we start bringing in those expensive little bundles of joy: Children!)*
• *Gifts to your Spouse*
• *Gifts to a Political Organization for its use.*

TIP: ACCEPT ALL GIFTS! "Thank you very much".

Mom's offer to pay for the reception was such a beautiful gesture. But, just in case this was too much for her, I wanted to prove I could pay for the reception. I pulled the remainder of Grandpa Wallace's portfolio out from under my chair. I held it up like a prized pig, saying, "Don't forget we have this resource, if needed."

Alan's wine glass stopped in mid-air. "How much is there?"

It hurt to remember what the investment used to hold. "Um, actually, I'm not sure."

He blinked a couple of times. "What do you mean, you're not sure?"

I shrunk a bit under his gaze. A finance addict should have her hot little fingers on all her investment numbers. "Well, losing 90% of it to Keith left a bad taste in my mouth. So, I had my bank hold the rest and then ... well ... I just put it away and forgot about it."

Alan sipped his wine, which seemed the proper response, since he knew how devastated I'd been by Keith. I could see a muscle flex in his jaw. I couldn't tell if he still wanted to slug the bastard or wrestled with the fact that I let a stock portfolio remain unattended.

My mother shook her head. "You know, Sam, it's been years, now. You could have a nice little nest-egg there, especially with the dividend reinvestment program that the Executor of the Estate set up."

"Wouldn't that be awesome?" I said.

I could feel that familiar thrill run up my spine at the thought of money earning interest on its own. Like any good addict, I tore open the portfolio. Let's see how I've done!

I still have 15% of the stock portfolio. My stomach clenched remembering that I let Keith talk me into liquidating the rest. What was I thinking? At the time of my divorce, the portfolio was worth $31,940 and looked something like this when I ignored it:

CSX Corp. (CSX), 100 shares, bought at $30.30, and paying a dividend of $0.40 per share for a total value of $3030.00. Coca-Cola

(KO), 100 shares, bought at $44.25, and paying a dividend of $1.24 per share for a total value of $4425.00. Johnson & Johnson (JNJ), 100 shares, bought at $55.50, and paying a dividend of $1.50 per share for a total value of $5550.00. Kimberly Clark (KMB), 100 shares, bought at $47.30 and paying a dividend of $1.96 for a total value of $4730.00. Merck (MRK), 100 shares, bought at $57.30, and paying a dividend of $1.52 for a total value of $5730.00. General Electric (GE), 200 shares, bought at $24.75, and paying a dividend of $1.12 per share for a total value of $4950.00. And, Exxon Mobil (XOM), 100 shares, bought at $35.25, and paying a dividend of $1.28 per share for a total of $3525.00. This bring the total value of my portfolio to: $31,940.00

Grandpa Wallace had originally picked these stocks because they were large companies that paid a dividend (which is a share of the profits), and he needed the income for his retirement expenses. The advice from the Executor of the Estate and the bank's financial department was to hold the stocks and use the money from the dividends to purchase more stock in the same company—the term they used was "reinvest". The bank's computer system automatically did this for me every time a dividend was received.

Alan took the portfolio and a slow grin came over his face. "Not bad for a neglected portfolio. But, I do hope you don't treat the house plants this way."

My mother pointed to the list. "Alan, what do all these terms mean? *And, why does CSX have 200 shares now. There were only 100 when Sam inherited it".*

Alan winked at me. "Do you want to tell her Sam, or should I?"

I laughed and waved him on. "Be my guest."

"Here's, a recap of the terms:

Dividend: *Is a share of the profits, or earnings of a company. Remember when you buy a stock; you are buying part of the company. If a company is profitable they will return part of your investment through a yearly amount, paid in quarterly installments.*

Stock Splits: *When a company has continued growth in the price of the stock, sometimes the Board of Directors and some shareholders* *will feel the price of the stock is too high. In order to make it more affordable the company will split the stock. The split does not create any new value for the shareholder; they still own the exact same percentage of the company. But, with the price in a more popular price range there is likely to be more buyers."*

This is what the portfolio looks like today—notice the adjustment for CSX stock splitting and the new shares purchased for all the companies from the dividend money.

CSX Corp. (CSX), 768 shares, trading at $20.30, and paying a dividend of $0.56 per share for a total value of $15,592.50 (Wow! This is great). Coca-Cola (KO), 126 shares, trading at $73.64, and paying a dividend of $2.04 per share for a total value of $9,278.64. Johnson & Johnson (JNJ), 131 shares, trading at $62.17, and paying a dividend of $2.44 per share for a total value of $8,144.27. Kimberly Clark (KMB), 135 shares, trading at $79.06 and paying a dividend of $2.96 for a total value of $10,673.10. Merck (MRK), 137 shares, trading at $37.37, and paying a dividend of $1.68 for a total value of $5,126.24. General Electric (GE), 271 shares, trading at $18.27, and paying a dividend of $0.68 per share for a total value of $4,962.43. And, Exxon Mobil (XOM), 126 shares, trading at $77.54, and paying a dividend of $2.28 per share for a total of $9,783.40. This bring the total value of my portfolio to: $63,560.58

A very nice profit of $31,620.58 or just shy of 100% - not too bad for an investment that has been neglected. I'll have to call the Executor and thank him.

CSX Corporation was a great winner, who would have thought a boring railroad company would do that well. The portfolio doubled, and luckily, only Merck went down and General Electric is even.

Jeeze, and to think, at the time, I thought the portfolio was old fashioned and boring—not one sexy high flying company in the mix. Look at the $31,620.58 profit, just think thirty-one thousand, six hundred and twenty dollars and I didn't have to do any work to earn it! I'm going to get more involved in this stock thing!!! For now though, I deserve a gift. White Jimmy Choo shoes for the most magical moment of my life! Of course, I'll take the money for the Jimmy Choos out of my checking account and not sell any of these stocks. Maybe I'll keep this portfolio forever (perhaps it would even earn back the Porsche Mr. Asshole got). Right after the wedding, I'm going to learn more about stock investing!

My heart swelled with pride that I could contribute. "See, Mom? I'd be happy to pay for our wedding."

"Absolutely not, Samantha Davis. Your reception is my gift to you. Don't you go spoiling it for me now just because you have your own private mint." The joy in my Mom's eyes was all I needed to see. After all, I had deprived her of a wedding when I eloped with … er, shithead.

Alan nodded in agreement. "Besides Sam, if we keep that portfolio in place, we'll have a good start for college tuition."

I looked at him, confused. "Are you going back to college?"

He laughed. "No, honey. Our kids!"

Mom actually got teary eyed. "I always wanted to be a Grandma!"

Kids. I'd dreamed of Alan as the father of my children since the first time I laid eyes on him. I couldn't believe my dream would come true. I raised my glass and said, "To Grandpa Wallace."

Alan winked. "To our future children."

A glint of mischief lit Alan's baby blue eyes and I could visualize a little boy with the same look. The pitter patter of little feet, and loving, small arms around me. Inquisitive little eyes. I had to shake myself from the moment. I smiled, and sipped my wine.

I watched Alan expertly work a cork from another bottle of Chardonnay, while the mischief in his eyes played out on his lips.

"Honey, I've been doing my homework. I can guarantee our first child will be a boy."

My Mother's mouth dropped open. Her shocked looked fell on me. I'd never heard this before, so I could only shrug.

"Come now, Alan. How can you possible guarantee the sex of a child?"

Alan refilled my glass grinning like a cocky rooster, the Chardonnay sounding like a tiny river bubbling into my glass.

He toasted me with his glass. "Don't you worry your little head about a thing, Darlin'. Daddy Al's got it all figured out. All we have to do is settle on his name".

For the first time I could remember, I sat there, speechless.

23

Aspen was the perfect place for our winter honeymoon, especially after our flawless (I refuse to remember it any other way) wedding and to-die-for reception in the Jade Room of the Waldorf Astoria. I will always love my wedding gown. The white mink surrounding my off-the-shoulder neckline felt divine!

Neither Alan nor I had ever been to Aspen, but our friends talked about how magnificent it was. Exploring the town together would make it our special place forever.

On our first night in Aspen, we had dinner at what the guidebook called "the most romantic restaurant in town" right in the heart of the beautiful old western village (well, it was western with a Gucci and Pucci flare). The owner, Josh, came over with the wine list and offered a few suggestions. Alan loved the list and they hit it off as if they'd known each other forever. Alan mentioned the word, 'collector', and Josh dragged us off to view his private wine cellar.

Cradling a dark bottle in his palms, Josh presented us with his first pride and joy. The uneven scrawl of letters looked like the vintner himself drank a few bottles before drawing the label. Alan and I practically knocked heads as we looked down at Josh's prize. He said, "This sweetheart cost me $8000. It's a 1989 Romanee-Conti. Solid. Very fine."

Stars lit Alan's eyes. Me? I just wanted to reach for a glass.

Josh slid another bottle from its cradle. His gaze moved from me, to Alan, to the bottle of wine like a proud papa. He practically whispered with reverence. "Chateau d'Yquem 1967 Sauternes. Best drunk between now and 2018."

"Have you tasted it?" Alan asked.

Josh shook his head. "This one's an investment. I bought it for $900. Sells on the market now for $1200. Not bad, eh?"

Alan eyed the bottle with new respect. "What are you going to do?"

"Wait a few years, then sell it."

I imagined the dark liquid on my tongue. "Or drink it."

He met my gaze with appreciation. "If I have a good year, I just might."

Alan slapped him on the back. "Be sure to invite us. We'll catch the first flight over."

We trailed Josh through his cellar as he pointed out desert wines that sell for $650, lovely Chardonnays for the mere price of $175 per bottle, Cabernets, Pinot Noirs, Champagne; he had them all by the case.

The man understood wine investments. By the few inches Alan floated off the ground, I knew he'd found a new love.

Now, if I could just keep him from drinking his investments!

That night in our room, he pulled out all sorts of graphs and articles Josh had given him to explain excellent wine investments. Then he logged onto the Internet to show me how serious wine investors could make huge profits. It was just too much fun!

The two major reasons to invest in wine are - I love the first one - *as an investment in future drinking. Buying young wines at the initial release price and storing them properly until they mature. And, second, a strictly financial investment - buying wines with the sole intention of reselling later for a profit. Just remember not to drink it!*

The global demand for fine wine, which is produced in very small quantities, has increased enormously over the last two decades. Wine can, and often has, outperformed the FTSE 100 and the Dow Jones, offering significant returns without the volatility of the stock market. I wonder if the stock traders would agree with this statement.

Alan's eyes lit up. "Sam, we have to learn about wine scores."

As a finance addict, I can't tell you what a turn on it was to have Alan kissing me in our honeymoon bed and talking about wine scores! Think I was a bit tipsy too! Alan pulled a report from beneath me—our honeymoon bed was covered with papers.

"Look. This guy, Robert Parker, developed a model to score wine based on the American High School system. That makes it easy. 85 -100 is good and anything below that is a C grade wine. But, there are other ways to describe wine scores. Look at this list, honey."

WA, is The Wine Advocate; WS the Wine Spectator magazine; MB is Michael Broadbent from *The Great Vintage Wine Book*; DE is Decanter magazine; GR is Gambero Rosso's journal on Italian wines; BH is Allen Meadows' Burghound.com; JR is Jancis Robinson on her site Purple Pages; ST is Stephen Tanzer: International Wine Cellar; and of course the famous RP is Robert Parker.

Scores are generally written as follows: RP 85 advising the consumer that Robert Parker has awarded the wine 85 points out of 100. Some wines have a range of points, for example: RP (85-90), and this is usually because the wine was tasted and scored before bottling and finishing.

He laughed. "Wouldn't it be fun to be Robert Parker and drink wine all day?"

We studied Wine Futures (also known as "En Primeur") which refers to buying wine after it is made, but before it is bottled. Cask samples of wines are made available for tasting to wine journalists and large wholesale buyers in the spring following the vintage. The wine is generally bottled and shipped around two years later.

The more Alan read, the more serious he became about investing in wines. "They should trade these futures in the commodity trading floors, because it's so much like all futures traded. Sam, look at this article on Bordeaux Futures. What a fabulous return. We should invest in this."

We also studied Bordeaux Futures which are commonly released in a number of "tranches" (literally 'slices' in French) with each release priced at a different level depending on how the previous one sold. 'Tranches' is a term also commonly used with mortgage-backed securities and we'll get into them in the next book, "Bonds Have More Fun".

1997 Bordeaux is an example of a poor vintage where the initial release was priced too high. The 1997s declined in price over the following years.

The Bordeaux 2000 vintage was quite the reverse, a vintage in great demand; it was initially priced too low. The first tranche prices did not appear on Wine-Searcher as the wine merchants reserved their allocations for their best customers. Even those who bought at the second or third tranche prices saw the value of their wines rise quickly.

We checked out the futures charts which we found at: http://www. wine-searcher.com/futures.lml the table shows a 25% to 36% increase in value in the first two years and a further 40% to 75% between 2003 and 2006 (an overall increase of between 100% and 150%), even at third tranche prices. Yummy!!

Alan rattled on about wine investment essentials, wine scores, wine futures, prices, abbreviations for wines used by merchants, fill levels, storage, how to recognize counterfeits, wine valuations, and insurance. Alan was falling fast, and I could understand why. Nothing is more alluring to a savvy bride on her honeymoon than the prospect of a lucrative new investment. I supported this idea of my gorgeous new husband one hundred percent. A financial maven is always looking for ways to be wealthier.

24

Back in New York, I had a few more days before returning to work, so I concentrated on moving into Alan's place. Alan's home is three times the size of mine with a great view of Central Park. Marital bliss could bloom here. Alan fully agreed with me that renting my condo ... or affectionately dubbed, 'the Hallway', was preferable to selling. Why sell an investment when you can get a tax write-off, and someone else to pay your expenses!

This was one of the reasons I bought my apartment when it converted to condominiums in the first place. Its location on the Upper East Side made it a terrific neighborhood for renting. And since the property was mine I took responsibility in handling the rental.

Of course, I'll rent my property at the highest rate the market will bear. Ideally, I want to cover my expenses and earn a tidy little profit, but at a minimum cover the expenses. So before placing several ads on the Internet, I posted a notice in the mailroom of my building and told my neighbors that I'd be renting the property. I figured word of mouth could get me a better referral than working with a stranger.

No matter what, however, I would spend the $25 on a credit check of my prospective renter and require a minimum of three referrals from sources such as present and past employers (to confirm income and *employment stability), as well as religious and civic associations who could vouch for the person's character.*

Then, to accept a one year lease, I'd require first and last month's rent plus the equivalent of one month's rent for security. This would be the perfect deposit. If I knew the tenant personally I might consider only requiring first month's rent and the security deposit.

Also, after the first year, if the tenant was ideal, I might offer the lease for two or three years. The good side to this is that you've locked a tenant in for the allotted time; the drawback is that you've locked your rent at a certain rate for the same time period. Sometimes the guaranteed rent is worth any loss in potential rent increases.

Basic Rental Agreements can be found on the Internet—just put 'rental lease agreement' into a search engine and choose the site you like best. Be sure to address who is responsible in case your renters need to leave for hurricanes, tornados, floods, etc.

Now, if I didn't want the headache of managing my rental, I could always engage a real estate agent or property manager to maintain the property. Real Estate Agents who are Certified Property Managers (CPMs) are certified by the Board of Realtors, and are required to adhere to a strict code of ethics. A property manager either receives a set fee for his/her services or a percentage of the monthly rent. This is negotiated between the owner and manager. In my case, the building has a handyman on staff, so my rental landlord life is much easier!

Property Management Agreements can also be found and downloaded from the internet.

Basically, the property manager will conduct the proper searches to approve a tenant, deposit monthly payments into your bank account, and handle any maintenance problems that occur. You do, however, have to pay any maintenance bills, unless previously agreed upon with the tenant.

Should the tenant eventually move out, or you decide to sell the property, or stop renting (foolish, unless you can afford to carry two properties!), adhere to the terms of the contract in releasing the tenant. Except for normal wear and tear, if the property is broom-swept and in the same condition as when occupancy was taken, the tenant should receive his full deposit (that had been held in escrow with the last month's rent, by the way.)

If damage has occurred to the apartment, you have a certain number of days (ideally 5-10 days) to repair the damage, deduct the amount from the security deposit (supply receipts, of course!) and refund the remainder of the deposit to the tenant.

Since I lived in the building for seven years, I already knew the superintendent and maintenance crew. So, maintaining the Hallway would be simple. I decided to lease the property on my own for now. Should life become too hectic, I'd engage a property manager later. Luckily, word of mouth worked. Within two weeks, a sweet girl from Long Island who'd just graduated from Parson s School of Design rented the Hallway for $200 more than my expenses.

Ah, what a rush knowing my real estate investment was sound, and that my money was making money for me!

Now, I, Samantha Davis-Abercrombie, headed for Tavern-On-The-Green in Central Park to meet Morgan for a drink before our husbands joined us for dinner. Morgan's husband, Todd, was late and Alan was investigating wine cellars.

All those delicious, dark bottles in the basement of Josh's restaurant had been singing a siren's song to my hubby ever since we returned from Aspen. I knew that by the time we got to bed tonight, we'd be negotiating how much square footage of our apartment we'd be dedicating to our next major investment, a wine cellar.

25

Oh my gosh, I'm pregnant!

That explains the cravings … and I thought working out at the gym had given me the enhanced cleavage! Holy smokes, we've only been married six months. Alan and I haven't even begun discussing his tried-and-true method for having a boy, so I'm pretty sure we're fifty-fifty on the outcome on this baby. Won't Alan be surprised!

Of course, this changes all of our budget and investment plans. Lucky for Alan, he already allocated $15,000 for his wine cellar, or I'd strongly suggest we cancel those plans. He's not going to like changing diapers in the wine tasting room, but oh well! Looks like the wine cellar will have to become part of the kitchen as I suggested. Obviously, we'll be staying with Mom in the mountains this summer instead a renting a place. Oh, and then we have to budget for our baby's education, hire a nanny, and most importantly, change our health insurance to include our new little bundle of love.

I think I need a nap already!

Then there's my job. I love my career. I plan to work through my pregnancy and then hire a nanny after my leave of absence. Ideally, I'd love to stay home with our baby. I'm lucky enough that I will be able to blend both worlds until our baby requires my full attention. I should be able take the baby and nanny with me on most traveling assignments. And, my boss will certainly permit me to work from home the lion's share of the time. I can count my blessings, because I have choices. Those mothers who have no choice and must work are today's heroes for balancing the tightrope walk of child-rearing and earning a living.

Here comes Alan and I can't wait to tell him!

He looks so handsome walking toward me, tall and rugged, just knowing a part of him was growing inside me sent shivers up my spine. One look and he knew something was up—am I that obvious?

He pulled me in his arms. "We're pregnant, aren't we?" He whispered.

I felt my eyes grow wide with surprise. "How did you know?"

He gave me that I-wanna-devour-every-inch-of-you look, letting his eyes rest on my breasts. He grinned. "First hint is that your shirts have become snugger."

I couldn't help but grin back. "You like?"

A soft growl escaped his throat. "Oh, honey, there's nothing about you I don't like. And, now, I'm going to get a little more."

He scooped me off the ground and twirled me in his arms before heading for the living room couch. "And, I don't even have to worry about getting you pregnant."

He captured my laughter with a kiss, wreaking havoc on my body with his hands, and in no time flat, laughter was the farthest thing from my mind.

I spent the next day searching the Internet and discovered that hiring a nanny entails legal ramifications as far as paying taxes and insurance, ensuring that they're eligible to work in the U.S. if not from this country, etc. The legal requirements alone for employing a nanny are enough to make a mother reconsider staying home! But, always one to face a challenge, I did my homework. I want to be prepared with all the facts for Alan ... he's going to have to give up the wine cellar after all.

If you go outside of an agency to hire your Nanny this is what you have to do. Fasten your seatbelt, because this is a complicated one! Here's what I learned:

Although a legal form of child care, nannies are not licensed by any regulatory agency. Nannies can be found through agencies, word of mouth, or through local colleges, religious organizations, etc. As the employer of a nanny, you must obtain federal and state employer identification numbers. For the federal number you need to fill out and return a Form SS-4. You can get this and all other federal tax forms from the Internal Revenue Service website www.irs.org or by calling (800) 829-3676. For your state number, call your state employment office. (Look under "Employment" in the state government listings in your phone book.)

www.nanny.org is a great website to walk you through the hiring details such as references, training programs, background checks and tax information.

The motherhood hormones were kicking into high gear and I forged on to make sure everything was taken care of before my sweet bundle of joy arrived. As if all of this Nanny information isn't enough. I dove right into researching prepaid college tuitions plans. You think birth is going to hurt? Wait until you see what colleges are asking for tuition these days. It's enough for a small mortgage!

Junior or Princess, as the case may be, is going to be an expensive little bugger. The sooner Alan and I begin the college planning process, the better. The government has designed plans to assist in saving for this time far off in the future. Of course, it's up to your child to qualify for the school, but we know any son or daughter of Alan's won't have to worry there. Heaven help him or her!

So, let's look at the 529 College Savings Plan:

Congress was thinking when they came up with this one. However, it is a State sponsored plan, and does vary slightly from state to state!! The tremendous benefits this plan offers are excellent for the person who owns it (which is not the child).

1. *No taxes are paid on the accounts earnings—how much interest and gains made.*
2. *There is no age limit as to when the monies have to be used.*
3. *The child has no control or access to the account.*
4. *If the child doesn't want to use the money, it can be rolled over to another family member.*

5. *Anyone can contribute to the account. (Of course, it's always more fun if the Grandparents just pay the tuition directly—see gifting section).*
6. *If your little genius gets a scholarship, the money can be withdrawn without incurring a penalty.*
7. *You can have a large income and still have this account.*

There are two options with this plan: a savings account or prepay tuition directly to a qualified educational institution at today's tuition rates. The most popular one is the savings account (junior might not like Daddy's alma mater). However, with tuition costs soaring, this might not be a bad way to go!

The savings account is set up by the State with an asset management company of the State's choice, the good news is you don't have to use the plan your state offers. Residency is not a requirement to set up a 529 Plan. You will be dealing directly with the asset management company—this can be done through an investment company or through your bank.

Like any investment it's best to shop around and find someone with whom you like to deal. We're still talking stocks and bonds here—just taking advantage of tax deferred earnings growth. The account itself is base makeup (just like a retirement account) and the investments are the rest of the makeup! Remember this plan is only as good as the investments inside it—carefully choose the stocks and bonds!

26

You'll be glad to know Alan's gorgeous blue eyes danced with delight every time he said, "We're pregnant."

He even shared in my cravings, eating ice cream and pickles, and diving into those tuna and pineapple sandwiches—not to mention, cheeseburgers with beets and onions. (I know. The thought makes me ill now.)

Of course, through my entire pregnancy, he continued to believe his sperm would never fail him and our baby would be a boy. Even in delivery, I still hadn't confessed what I'd known for months:

We were having a girl.

Watching the expectation and concern in Alan's eyes only compounded my guilt. I had to tell him. Or act like I just didn't know. But, I couldn't play dumb. I was too honest. So, I had to 'fess up. And soon.

As if to prod me on, another labor pain hit.

I clutched Alan's hand. "This one's a doozie!"

"Ouch, Sam! You're breaking my fingers."

"Honey." Pant. Pant. "If it's a girl … " Pant. Pant. "Will you still love me?"

He grimaced in pain. "We can have a monkey and I'll be okay if you don't break my hand." His fingertips were turning purple.

The spasm lessened and I released my grip. Before closing my eyes, I glimpsed Alan shaking his hand to engage circulation and he looked really pale.

"Are you okay?"

"Just worried for you, Sam. You know I'd go through this for you if I could. Just hang in there!"

I lay there now understanding why kids are spoiled rotten. After the pain of childbirth, mothers are terrified their babies will try to crawl back inside and do it again. So they give them everything they want!

With closed eyes I said, "Thanks, Alan. I can do this—it just hurts like hell!" I managed a chuckle. "We're having a girl."

Silence.

I opened one eye. "Alan?"

He stared at his hands. "I'm not feeling so good."

"Because we're having a girl?" I wondered aloud.

He looked shocked. "Hell, no. I'm just ... feeling kinda nauseous."

I nodded and swiped perspiration from my lip. "Why don't you go to the waiting room?"

More silence. I closed my eyes. It was only seconds before the next contraction. I reached for his hand.

Nothing.

"Alan?"

He'd escaped to the door, beckoning a nurse to attend me. "Be right back, Sweetie. I have to hit the john."

Kelly entered the world with her beautiful night-blue eyes blinking in surprise against the delivery room lights, her lips pursed like a rosebud. She didn't even whimper. They laid her on my belly. I knew I'd just experienced a miracle. Going back to work would be the hardest sacrifice I'd make. I wanted nothing more than to spend the rest of my days coddling this amazing bundle of joy. Oh, the little baby sounds she was making! And her little movements outside my stomach were once so familiar inside.

Alan barreled in five minutes after the fact looking much better.

He did make up for missing his daughter's birth, though. With just a glance at her sweet, little face, he bundled her into his arms, cooing like a fool as she wrapped him around her precious little finger.

Yep. Kelly was the new love in his life.

I found out later, that while Kelly made her debut, Alan wasn't ill. He'd been on the phone with the wine merchant buying 20 cases of Reserve to celebrate our daughter's arrival into the world. My labor had set him into a panic, so he went investing. What a chicken!

Men.

No wonder women get to have the babies.

Our life changed with the birth of Kelly; for better and for worse. The better, of course, was her presence. Her little sweep of blond hair, rosy cheeks and sweet smelling skin made holding her irresistible. Those saucer-sized eyes were still dark blue, but their shape was mine. A momma always likes to see something of herself in her daughter.

The worst was how fast my three month leave of absence flew by. It practically took that long to find a good nanny. The Nanny's expenses were $540 per week! However, that little chunk of change didn't affect Alan's wine collection. Oh, no. He argued that a man with a highly visible job, such as his, needed the satisfaction of coming home at night, enjoying a good meal and appreciating the investment of all those fine wines chilling behind the smoked glass doors of his wine cellar—like viewing a collection of rare art.

Van Gogh and Monet, eat your heart out!

Lucky for me, Alan enjoyed his meals with Kelly cradled in the crook of his arm. He had as much trouble keeping away from her as I.

Our nanny arrived a month before I had to return to work so we could adjust to each other. She had worked for five years in another home with two small children. She came highly recommended, appeared well groomed, competent, and required room and board. I felt angst for maybe half a minute as I cleared out my home office to accommodate her. It wasn't so bad cramming my desk into our bedroom, but no matter how big the apartment, our privacy disappeared.

That was the worst of all.

No more sex on the dining room table.

Back at work, Mr. Mozel granted me company stock options as an incentive to stay on board. Stock options are a marvelous addition to one's portfolio even though some consider them 'golden hand cuffs'. *A stock option is the right to purchase (in financial language it is called a 'call'—think of calling the stock to you) or sell (in financial language a 'put'- think of putting stock down) a stock. An employee stock option is always a call, and is the right to purchase company stock for a predetermined period of time. It's used as a form of non-cash compensation. My Mozel options were issued at today's stock price and would take three years to vest, so if I were to leave the company before that they'll be no good.* But, I love my job and with this incredible nanny, there should be no problem balancing hubby, baby and worky.

I'll discuss trading stocks later on. So stay tuned!

Meanwhile, back at the ranch, I guess the lack of privacy didn't really keep Alan and me from jumping each other's bones, because I'm pregnant again. Alan had me taking my temperature every morning with a basal thermometer, and he kept better track of my ovulation than I did. He said taking my temperature was the tried-and-true method to conceive a boy. All we had to do was have wild sex within twelve hours of the morning my temperature dropped.

Okay. So, we did, and it wasn't wild monkey sex. Actually, I may still have been sleeping … but it worked!

Holy smokes.

Months of exercise to get our bodies back into shape just shot down the tubes. (Yes, Alan ate all those cartons of Haagen Daz right along with me.) I thought we were just practicing. Kelly's only eight months old. Wait until Mister Super Sperm hears this news!

Now we're really going to run out of room.

Uh-oh. If we have to move, Alan won't want to leave his wine cellar behind. Maybe we can buy the apartment next door and knock out a wall. I wonder if our neighbors are happy living there …

27

Despite loving my job, and working from home a few days each week, the thought of full time employment and raising two children became daunting. However, other mothers far more hard-pressed than I were managing quite well juggling their lives. What broke the proverbial camels back for me was my nanny.

There we were one evening, Alan and I, watching a news documentary on the nanny brigade whisking daily through Central Park, and what did the camera pan? My nanny under a tree kissing some freak with old tattoos while Kelly sat crying, unheeded, in her stroller. You should have seen the color drain from the nanny's face when we re-played the documentary for her.

Time was up. The nanny gig was over. I took the parental reins. It took all of twenty minutes to contact her agency, reference the TV station where they could access the documentary, fire the irresponsible ninny and send her packing without ripping every hair out of her head.

Now, I needed a solution or was doomed to give two weeks notice and leave my stock options behind. I called Mom immediately. She agreed to move in with us until I finished my time with Mozel. Alan decided my second pregnancy, firing the nanny, and finally leaving work to become a stay-at-home mom offered enough incentive to celebrate. He raided the wine cellar and popped open a delightful cabernet, circa 1964.

How sweet. I'm pregnant. I get to watch him drink it.

Of course, once my life changed, so did some of my investments. *First, I needed to transfer my 401(k) to a 'rollover' IRA, and I repeated the process exactly as I had after leaving the law firm for Mozel (see Chapter 8).* And, now that I was no longer employed, Alan added Kelly and me to his health insurance. Mozel held a beautiful bon voyage party for me, leaving a door open should I ever wish to return. That gesture alone gave me the confidence to tackle my new life and my tighter budget.

Little did I know how badly I'd need that confidence.

By the time our son, Luke (yes, Alan's method worked), entered the world, all hell broke loose with Alan's job. Remember when Alan and I first met and he told me how cut-throat his business was? Well, his prediction came home to roost. I hate to say he was demoted, but … he was demoted. Being passed over for a promotion at the ripe age of 43 in his world, is a demotion, any way you look at it. Those young, hungry wolves snapping at his heels had their way—the new young, athletes were coming in. Of course, that meant our income would stay the same, but now we have more mouths to feed. The word, budget, took on a deeper meaning.

Alan's solution to this setback?

Move to Napa Valley and buy a vineyard!

The only, major problem with that logic was our $200,000 wine investment had been slowly dwindling. I suspected those select cabernets and delectable zinfandels may have had something to do with Alan's work performance. I wasn't ready to use the word alcoholic, but it haunted my dreams. I'm no dummy (any more). Alan remained loving and attentive and hard-working, but stress does take its toll. Stock brokers and traders are notorious for becoming addicted to one stimulus or another to relieve their frayed nerves.

So, I nixed the idea of a vineyard. (Can you imagine what Alan's liver would eventually look like if he owned a freaking winery?)

But, I did see the wisdom in moving.

Time had come to leave the city. Its sky-high taxes, insurance and general cost of living with two infants was draining our income. I began my search immediately. What we would save in city taxes alone should more than make up for the cost of little mouths to feed, well at least while they were young.

Now, if Alan didn't lose his job completely, we'd still have health insurance coverage and a steady income to keep us in the pink. (Black, technically, but too dark a color for me.)

As you can imagine, I searched high and low for mortgage information.

I reviewed my notes from the purchase of my 'hallway'. Am I the only person in the world who's bought a hallway? It is really cute! The girl renting it painted it light pink and bought a pink couch to match—too fun. Anyway, I digress. The information for mortgages hasn't changed; only the interest rates have (review Chapter 18). I'm going to push Alan for a fixed rate mortgage this time because interest rates are low, but the news says they are expected to go up soon. I'm going to speak with the lender about refinancing my 'hallway' too—maybe I can save some money on the monthly payment.

We carefully searched the real estate market, home prices and mortgage rates before deciding on a house. As expected, the rule for home buying is LOCATION, LOCATION, LOCATION. We found the perfect home in Connecticut—nowhere near Keith, I can assure you. Alan agreed to trade the long commute to the city for the lower income taxes in the suburbs. Plus there is a yard for the kids to play outside!

Any trepidation I had about changing our lives evaporated when all the pieces fell into place. No sooner did I find our new home, than the perfect couple appeared to buy our apartment. Of course, he was a stock broker and fell in love with Alan's wine cellar. His lovely wife just smiled, and said, "We'll take it."

I love it when life works out so smoothly!

Since we file our taxes jointly, upon selling the apartment, we could claim up to $500,000 of the gain a capital gains exemption from our taxes. We didn't quite make half a million in profit, but we did gain

$367,242.87, which we immediately used for the new house. Luckily, we made a profit and not a loss on the sale. Any money lost cannot be deducted from taxes at all.

The closing on our house was delayed when the title company found an issue with some plumber who put a lien on the house. *That's the beauty of a title search on prospective home purchases. If a contractor isn't paid for work done, he can demand payment from the seller prior to the sale of the house. The title search insures that you, the buyer, do not get hit with such an expense.* But, once we closed, nothing slowed the move. I coordinated the packing and moving while breastfeeding, cooking, canceling and/or forwarding utility bills and other accounts. Alan made arrangements for the wine to be shipped under refrigeration, while hiring a new architect to build an even larger wine cellar in our shiny new basement.

A nightmare? Yes, but all of it was worthwhile.

I wanted Alan to be happy. Besides, I couldn't wait to see the kids running around our humongous back yard, even if it would take a while longer. Kelly was walking, but Luke, not yet. He still gurgled, messed his diaper and offered endless entertainment for his sister who now had a real live doll of her own!

Once we'd settled in, and Alan acclimated to the commute, I finally caught my breath. The following months were sheer nirvana. Not until one really quiet morning, with the birds chirping outside my window and the sun streaming in, did I realize that in between changing diapers, creating our new home and grocery shopping, my professional edge had become soft.

Something was missing, and I couldn't quite put my finger on it. Yet.

28

Don't get me wrong. I was happy. Deliriously happy! Even Alan seemed to be basking in the glow of our new life. He even managed to refurbish the wine cellar without drinking the investments. But, when the kids napped and everything was quiet, I realized I missed the adrenaline rush of landing accounts or hopping a plane for a trade show in Italy. I needed to channel my professional talents to keep myself whole.

Of course, the answer came to me while folding laundry and watching Good Morning America on TV. A Huggies commercial caught my eye. I'd been potty training Kelly, and they say boys are harder to train than girls, so any help would be a huge welcome. Huggies had developed a pull up training pant with "Cool Alert."

What's that you ask?

Cool Alert is some sort of lining in the Huggies that turns cool against the baby's skin when they piddle. In turn, the change in temperature prompts the toddler to say something or make a face and the attentive care giver knows it's a potty training opportunity.

Clever, eh?

So, I thought to myself, how many potty trainers are there in America at this moment? And if all their care givers bought these cool training pants, then Huggies would make a fortune. Which led to the next thought.

Wonder what their stock is doing?

I'd like to say I came to this clever conclusion myself, but no. I'd become friendly with a woman down the block with a daughter Kelly's age. And lo and behold, she'd confided that out of boredom, she taught herself how to trade stocks on the Internet.

I thought, "If Emily can trade stocks, why can't I? And, I had wanted to learn more about stocks before I got married and had kids. Perfect timing!"

So, I turned 'Good Morning America' off, and focused on getting more information.

Now Emily told me she began trading by checking Yahoo, Google and TDAmeritrade's pages. So, I did the same. What a jumble! (Remember, stocks are ownership in a company, as explained in Chapter 6.) So, like a good finance addict, I knew money knowledge was an adrenaline rush. I pressed on for more investment websites.

Here's what I discovered:

If you just jump in and start trading you can get killed. Well, not literally killed—like there's not going to be blood everywhere or anything, but you could lose your money, which for a finance addict, is the same thing. And, we'd all rather have a new pair of shoes than lose money. So, keep in mind the object is to make money … hopefully, a lot of money … or, at least enough to buy a new, guilt-free outfit, accessories and all.

Stocks (equity) will look like chaos at first sight. But, when you start breaking down the information into manageable pieces, the logic becomes clear. So, that's what we're going to do with stock trading: break it down one level at a time.

Okay, think about it this way: You go to your best friend's house. She's married, has five kids and when you walk through the door all you see is chaos. You suggest she could use one of your amazing fruit smoothies for an energy boost. At her tired, but contented grin, you head for the kitchen for the blender and the ingredients.

Whoa. The kitchen is like a war zone. But you soon realize that it's organized chaos. The toys are in the southwest corner, the children's dishes are on the near counter, the adult dishes are on the far counter and all electronics are in the cabinet above the sink. Of course, the smoothie ingredients are in the fridge.

Now, let's translate that into searching the stock market for a company that has good earnings, potential growth, and is not too expensive. Everything is where it should be, but at first glance, it's just another mess.

Our kitchen is the stock quote—very easy once you break it down.

Okay, like looking for the blender, let's look at companies that produce everyday items, *Huggies (KMB), Pampers (PG), toothpaste (CL, CLX, PG), make-up (AVP, REV, LORL), food storage, (TUP, NWL), etc. Once you pick a company, the first thing to do is pull up a stock quote on the Internet. All the major search engines offer stock quotes, just click on the tab that says 'finance' and enter the quote on the next screen. If you don't have the symbol, go to the look up tab and type in the name of the company.*

Pull up a stock quote for Tupperware (TUP).

Are you thinking to yourself, Tupperware?!? My Grandmother bought Tupperware. I haven't seen or heard of a Tupperware party in years. But, we're looking for good investments—not sexy stock(ing)s. So, I conduct a search on Tupperware, the company. Here's what I found:

Tupperware bought Sara Lee's beauty line.

They are launching "spa parties" in the US.

They own over 2,000 'party locations' in China, having recognized that homes are too small for gatherings. These 'party locations' are now like sorority houses for the Chinese consumer and their sales numbers reflect really fun events.

And, wait until Bono hears about this one: Tupperware is changing the world. They have a whopping two (2) million plus direct salespeople worldwide and most of them are women. Promoting and teaching entrepreneurship around the globe. It has been called the

"Tupperware effect" because the women create businesses which create wealth, which in turn help the entire community and eventually the entire country.

Again, we're in our best friend's kitchen (the stock quote), and while the blender (Tupperware) looks old, it really has the best small engine technology known to man. A good investment in the long run!

Now, before we look at the kitchen (the quote) in detail, let's take a peek at how the market works. *A key fact to remember is: there is* **always a buyer and a seller**. *Remember Economics 101. Something is only worth what someone else is willing to pay for it.*

Think: Saks Fifth Avenue. Items placed "On Sale" at Saks are items no one willingly bought at full price. Saks will keep lowering the price until the item moves. Wall Street basically works the same way. For every trade, there is someone on the other side willing to pay a price.

Get it?

I knew you would! Are you starting to tingle yet?

With stock trading, someone is always keeping the flow of the market going (sometimes it's a computer program). Buyers and Sellers are brought together and coordinated by traders/computers. Of course, traders designed the computer programs, so it's just like a live trader in super-fast motion.

The next fact to remember is once again, language. Remember when Morgan taught me that learning finance was like learning another language? Once you've mastered the jargon, you become a finance wiz. Well, the same holds true once more with stock trading. *And dig this: the* **trade language is ALWAYS from the point of view of the Trader**. *If the Trader is selling the stock it's called ASK (what the trader is 'asking' for the stock), and you are buying. In reverse, if the Trader is buying the stock, this is the BID (think 'b' for buying), and you are selling.*

Oh, hold on. Kelly just woke up from her nap. I'm going to get her a snack and a juice box. Why don't you take a minute to make a cup of tea or get a cool drink and meet me back here in five minutes? I can't wait to tell you more!

She's so cute in her little pink jumpsuit with the bunnies on it!

Okay, ready? Let's work on more trading language. You can pull up a TUP, Tupperware quote on any investment site and it should contain the same information. I'll explain what each of the terms mean. I guarantee that once you get familiar with the terms, you'll be absolutely fabulous at reading stock quotes. You're going to love me for this one!

The first item listed is LAST TRADE. This number constantly changes throughout the day as buyers and sellers come together. The price represents the last time the stock was purchased/sold. The arrow indicates whether the public bought or sold. If the arrow is up the public bought and if the arrow is down the public sold. So, if your screen is flashing an up arrow (usually green also), there are buyers out there and chances are the stock is going up. Please note, not all quotes offer this function.

Why is this important?

Because you need to know whether there are more buyers than sellers. Economics 101: if there are more buyers the price will go up. If there are more sellers, the price will go down.

See?

Next, DAYS RANGE: The price range that the stock traded in that day. Where is the price right now? High? Low? Medium?

TRADE TIME: The time of the last trade. Sounds simple, but this is where the Internet gets you! Basic on-line trading is 15-30 minutes delayed, and more sophisticated computer trading is "real time". If you're buying and holding your stock, it's no big deal. However, if you're actively trading, it makes a huge difference.

52 WEEK RANGE: What the stock price has done in the last year. Are you buying at the high? Medium? Low?

CHANGE: How much the price moved from the previous night's close. The amount is indicated. The up or down arrow tells in which direction the amount ended. Oh, and in case there's no arrow, the price color is the indicator. If the price color is green, the price is up. If red, the price is down. This number also changes throughout the day. Think: CNBC "Coca-Cola was down 79 cents in late day trading due to questions with the China bottlers."

VOLUME: How many shares have been traded that day.

AVERAGE VOLUME: This number indicates how many shares are normally traded in a day. These two volume figures matter because you need to know two things.

1. *Is the stock liquid? Meaning: Are there enough shares traded in a day so you can easily sell your position if needed? If you own 2000 shares and 5000 shares is the daily volume, you could get stuck if bad news comes out and everyone wants to sell.*

2. *Are an inordinate amount of shares being bought/sold that day? If so, do you know why? Wall Street is full of rumors. And just like the mean girls in high school, not all of them are true.*

PREVIOUS CLOSE: What the stock finished at the night before. They are doing the math for you (love it when other people do the math!). Previous close plus or minus change = last trade. Elegant in its simplicity!

OPEN: What the stock opened at - - and yes, it would seem this would be the same as the previous close. However, this number is important because something could have happened over night which caused the price to move in Tokyo, Singapore, Hong Kong, Paris, Frankfurt, or London, or the company could have announced earnings, which is the primary thing that would trigger a difference. (We'll get into earnings later. No worries.) Remember: at the end of our day, Tokyo is opening for the following day. Lots of trading can occur while we sleep.)

MARKET CAP: Translation: Market Capitalization. The price the stock is trading at times how many shares are outstanding. In other words, what the company is worth.

Remember in Chapter Seven at my first job when I was making decisions for my 401(k) investments? I looked at Large Cap and Small Cap Funds. Large Cap typically means companies with a $2 billion and above market cap. Investors use this number for several reasons. The most important reason is risk. The larger the company the less volatile the price, in other words, the risk of losing money is typically smaller. A Small Cap company is more risky, or more the price has a higher chance of going down. Most start-up firms have very small market caps and are more risky.

Clear? I'm sure it is. You're doing beautifully absorbing all of this into your brain. Ah, my very smart student, you make me proud!

*Next, BID: The price at which the Trader is willing to buy the stock. In other words, the Bid is the **price you can sell** the stock. Remember, from the Trader's point of view: Bid—b is for buying.*

*ASK: The price at which the Trader is willing to sell the stock. So, it's the **price you can buy** the stock. Remember: Asking. The price the Trader is asking you to pay.*

P/E: Translation: Price to Earnings ratio. How much the price is compared to the earnings per share. The 'last trade' divided by the earnings per share. Why is this important? It is a great number to use for comparison purposes to other company's stock prices. (It gets more complicated than this, but we'll leave it here for now.)

EARNINGS PER SHARE: How much the company earns per share, and it's an excellent indicator of how well the company is doing. Imagine starting a Hair Salon, you have to buy shampoo, hire stylists, a receptionist and rent space. It takes awhile before you pay off all of the startup costs. So, after everyone is paid the amount left over is the earnings. In stocks, we just divide the earnings by the shares.

1Y TARGET EST.: Translation: One year target estimate or the price analysts think the stock will be at in one year. Analysts are usually pretty good at determining this estimate. The proof is in their income since they can earn up to a million dollars a year. Not bad, eh?

DIV & YIELD: The first number is the dividend—indicated on a per share basis. So, if the dividend is $0.88, you earn 88 cents per year for every share you own. So, if you own 200 shares ($0.88 x 200) your dividend would be $176 per year. The yield is the percentage of the "Last Trade" number, and primarily used for comparison purposes: 3.8% is an excellent yield for a stock because you not only get this dividend and yield, but you also get the potential growth in the price of the company.

CHART: Pull up any yearly chart on the Internet. Notice how the price bounces around? This will also be the case for the daily, weekly, and monthly charts—we are looking for a general curve to the upside. Charts are also useful for picking a price to buy or sell. Women tend to be excellent chart readers. We are naturally good at picking out patterns (goes back to caveman days, gathering, tending the hearth and being aware of predators)—it's really easy to tell if a chart is going up or down by looking at all of the patterns.

Now, pull up any five year chart on the Internet. The top portion of the chart indicates the trade prices and the bottom is the volume. Do you see the pattern? Is the chart going up or down? What about the volume—see the spikes and how the stock moves? Real news, rumor, earnings?

BETA: A comparison used to determine how much the stock trades with the benchmark. So a beta of 1 means the stock trades exactly as the market does, and 1.5 means it is more volatile than the market. How much risk will you take? Would you spend a hundred dollars on the four inch wide black belt? Or would the $20 version be better, because it'll be out of style in a month—I'd say that belt will have a beta of 4!

NOW, LET'S GO SHOPPING!

29

We girls are going to use our well-honed, expert shopping skills to go stock shopping. There are thousands of companies out there! Let's only look at those we like. So, let's make a girlfriend deal: if we find a stock we don't like, we'll just move onto the next company. (If only finding a boyfriend was that simple!)

Speaking of Huggies versus Pampers, Luke needs to be changed.

What did he eat today? YUCK!

While I was busy cleaning Luke, my sweet Kelly brought me one of her sippy cups filled with water.

"Here. Mommy's thirsty," she said in her very cute voice.

I make an effort to keep the children hydrated so felt I had to set a good example. I took the cup. "Why thank you, honey!"

I drank the cool liquid, not realizing how thirsty I had been. I handed the cup back to her. "Mmmm. That was good. Now, let me finish with Luke's diaper."

She scampered off. "More!"

I buttoned up Luke and bundled him into a big hug. I love the baby-soft smell of his hair. But, enough mothering. Let's get back to trading stocks.

First, a product you like might be in the development stage but that's okay (don't forget to really understand the risk with all investments). It's not a good idea to pick stocks based on good-looking CEO's!

(Of course, if we'd all picked Apple based on Steve Job's good looks we'd be reading this book in a Jacuzzi while drinking champagne on our yacht off the Cote d'Azur.

Our deck steward, Job (he couldn't possibly have another name), would ask, "Samantha, are you having a nice time? Captain Johan would love you to join him for dinner tonight".

"Thank you, Job, YES, how could I not be having a wonderful time! We would love to dine with the Captain tonight, I so enjoy his stories, conversation and laughter, not to mention what fabulous command he has of the seas. And please ask Gideon for another glass of Champagne, Rose, if we have it. I'm sure Alan is somewhere chatting with him about life, travel and his knowledge of wine. You all are such an amazingly interesting crew".

But, oh how I digress! Out of the Jacuzzi and back to stocks).

Really, though, we're seeking solid information, nothing flashy.

If you're not sure where to look for companies, great sources are: new products friends are trying, everyday goods, Wired magazine, blog sites, any/all newspapers, etc. In the spirit of our earlier analogy, don't be afraid to dig through the chaos to find where the blender is hiding.

Second point while searching for a company: is there room for growth? We want to buy low and sell high, like finding a great sale at our favorite store.

Answer these questions:
- ✓ *Is the last trade less than the one year target estimate? The target estimate is what the analyst's very complex models say the stock will rise to—so, we want this number to be substantially more than the current price.*
- ✓ *Is the chart going up or down? A very simple, but important question that my mentor constantly asked me. We want the chart to be going up!!*
- ✓ *Is the P/E in line with the rest of the sector (compare diapers to diapers)? There shouldn't be that much difference between Proctor*

& Gamble (Pampers) and Kimberly Clarke (Huggies). If the P/E's have a big difference, there is potential for the smaller one to increase, i.e. the stock price to go up. This is a great way to make extra money for shoes and handbags!

✓ *Check the volume—is there enough volume to easily move in and out of shares?*

✓ *Earnings per share—are they positive or negative? Newer companies will put all earnings back into the company to spur growth. The upside could be greater; however the downside could also be greater. So, for large mature companies we want greater earnings per share and for smaller start-up companies less is okay. We're looking for a ramp-up in earnings, as the company grows the earnings get better.*

✓ *Be careful—as you would in all financial matters. Shopping for stocks can be tons of fun, and just like hitting the sales at the mall, pick, choose, and compare carefully.*

Oops. Another break here. Kelly bee-lined for me once again, carefully balancing another cup of water.

"Here, Mommy!"

Her bright eyes were ever so thrilled with her delivery. I couldn't help but accept the sippy cup and make a big show of drinking the water.

Then, it occurred to me. Kelly can't reach the kitchen sink. Or any sink for that matter. A really gross feeling filled my stomach.

"Kelly, where'd you get the water?"

She beamed. "In there."

My eyes narrowed suspiciously as she pointed down the hall.

Where, honey?"

I stood, scooped up Luke and followed her.

Don't you know the little rascal led me right to the powder room off the kitchen, dipped her sippy cup into the toilet, and held the cup up to me.

"Here's more, Mommy!" She began to drink some.

With lightening speed I captured the cup from her hand not wanting to frighten her. As the fact that I just consumed two cups of toilet water registered, my disgust dissolved into belly laughs.

"Oh, kitten, we don't drink from the toilet!"

The surprise in her eyes morphed into confusion. "Chester does."

I shook my head. "Chester is a dog. Grandma doesn't mind if he drinks from her toilet. People drink water from the sink. Okay?"

Boy, did I burst her bubble. But, hey, bubbles are meant to be burst! The dot-com bubble, the real estate bubble, currency, stock bubbles. The Dutch are still waiting for the price of tulips to come back. And, the bubbles churning in my stomach didn't feel so good, either! Oh, the joy of parenting. I can't wait until Daddy comes home to hear this one!

But, all is settled now. Kelly is more than happy to play with Legos at my feet while Luke watches from his carrier.

Now, where were we? Oh, yes. I love the idea of trading stocks and potentially earning income while raising these kiddies of mine.

My neighbor, Emily, told me a professional stock-broker friend of hers says there's a Wall Street joke that goes like this: "The quickest way to make $10 million trading at home is to start with $20 million." In other words, it's really easy to lose money if you're not careful. So, begin investing with only a small amount or use imaginary money. Try trading with this "mad money" just for fun. Once you understand the market, then you can seriously invest. Promise me you'll not go hog-wild the first time testing your stock-trading wings. Okay?

Good.

Now, let's trade stocks!

Remember the different markets from Chapter Eight? New York Stock Exchange, NASDAQ, American Stock Exchange and there are markets around the world with which we'll deal with later because we don't need them, yet. Some traders would say we'd never need them, but we love the rest of the world! Parlez-vous Francais? I can't wait to take the children to France!

Back to stocks. *There are three ways to trade stocks:*

One, at home through the Internet, many sites are available which will let you set up an account. The good news is that this process is relatively easy and quick to set up. The down side is that you're basically on your own and the information/quotes are delayed from 15- 30 minutes. If you want to simply buy and hold stocks, or you already have an existing portfolio and want low fees, this is the strategy for you.

Two, trade at home through an advanced trading service (also on the computer). This service will cost a monthly fee. Bloomberg is the most sophisticated at $5000 per month and the services go down from there in both sophistication and price to around $50 per month. If you're willing to spend all of your time trading, studying stocks and keeping abreast of the markets, this strategy is the one for you.

Three, you could go through a broker-dealer, like Charles Schwab, Morgan Stanley, UBS, Wells Fargo, Bank of America, etc. My Mother used to tell me, "Two minds are better than one". If you find a broker you like (perhaps even through your bank), or if you would prefer the benefits of a large company conducting your research, I would recommend this strategy. You can still trade on-line at a fraction of the cost, but you have the added benefit of a larger company. And, it's always nice to have someone with whom to voice your questions, ideas and concerns.

EXCELLENT ADVICE FROM PROFESSIONAL TRADERS:

✓ *When you're down 10% - get out. If your stock decreases in value 10% from the original investment—sell, get out! Don't mess around—you want to be able to invest tomorrow. A sell strategy is as important as a buy strategy.*

✓ *Do not marry a stock. (By the way, women are much better at this than men.) Get rid of it!*

✓ *Do not throw good money at a bad investment. The whole concept of 'doubling down' is not used by people who own mansions, yachts and jets. If you get out when you're 10% down you don't have to try to recoup money when you're 50% down.*

✓ *When you're down 10% - get out. Yes, I said this a second time.*

✓ *Keep the 'mood of the crowd' in mind when deciding to buy or sell. A stock is half reality, and half fantasy, with the fantasy being the 'mood of the crowd' (think: dot-com). In the frenzy of the dot-com* *years, people would pay $100 for a stock worth $10. No designer purse is that hot. Well, okay, the Hermes Berkin bag might be worth it. I don't own one—do you?*

✓ *If you buy and then sell the stock because it went down 10%, keep it on your radar. You originally bought it for a good reason and perhaps it will have potential down the road.*

✓ *When you're down 10% - get out. Yes, this fact is important enough to repeat three times!*

BUYING OR SELLING STOCKS

Okay, now you've decided to purchase a stock, you like the research, price and think there is potential for growth. So, it's time to order the shares.

This can be done in two ways: a Market Order or a Limit Order.

*A **Market Order** tells the trader you want to buy the shares. Shares are usually sold in lots of 100. Any amount less could cost more in commission. So, a nice round number is usually the way to buy 100, 200, 300 etc). The trader will execute the order at the price and time they see fit—this is not good for you! You will probably pay a higher price! A higher price is okay if the market is moving up and you just want the shares, or if you're going to hold the shares for so long it won't matter in 5 years.*

*A **Limit Order** tells the trader at what price you'd like to purchase the stock. The amount of money between the Bid and Ask is called the spread. This amount of spread is the flexibility the trader has in raising or lowering the price for that timeframe (which is usually measured in seconds because the market is moving). If the ask is 30.85 and the bid is 30.05 the spread is $0.80, the trader is willing to sell the stock for $30.85 to you. However, if you're only willing to pay $30.15 for the stock you send the trader a message through a 'limit order' indicating this. Chances are good you'll get the shares for the lower price.* Now if we could only do this at Jimmy Choo we'd all be much happier wearing those expensive shoes.

And that's Stock Trading 101. You bought your first stock. Congratulations! How's the adrenaline rush???

Oh! And, here's my little Princess coming to see me. I have to sing to her—she's so cute! Join in:

"The itsy bitsy spider went up the water spout,
Down came the rain, and washed the spider out.
Out came the sun and dried up all the rain.
Then the itsy bitsy spider went up the spout again!"

Don't forget about SPDR's (Standard & Poors 500 Deposit Receipt— pronounced spiders), it is traded like a regular stock, designed to track the value of the S&P 500 (symbol: SPY), and pays a quarterly dividend. It is considered an Exchange Traded Fund (ETF). There are many other types of ETF's that track different indexes, sectors, etc. For example, on NASDAQ the PowerShare QQQ (symbol: QQQQ) and many international ETF's. It is worth looking into, as the diversification is high and the commission is low. And, don't forget, buy low and sell high!

Let's hit the wine cellar and grab a great bottle of Montrachet to celebrate!

Alan has a business dinner tonight and won't be home until about 9:30pm. Perhaps I'll surprise him with my new purchase from Victoria's Secret and light candles in the bedroom. Yummy!

In the meantime, do you know the story of the Montrachet family? It's a fun story. Monsieur Montrachet purchased a large tract of land in the Cote de Beaune subregion of Burgundy, France, and started growing grapes. His wine became very popular as news of his talents as a vintner spread. He married and his wife bore one son and two daughters. Upon his death he bequeathed the best part of his vineyard to his son, and this wine became known as Chevalier-Montrachet. He gave two equal parts of the vineyard to each daughter, Puligny and Chassagne. Then, unknown to the family, he had a son from another woman to which he left the least valuable of the land. This son, having a sense of humor, named his wine, Batard, which is French for bastard. So, the four great Montrachet wines, Chevalier, Puligny, Chassagne and Batard, continue on to this day, and they really are great white wines. It's like drinking spun gold!!!

30

I t's been three years and I think Alan is jealous.

Yeah. Looks like trading stocks comes naturally to me. I've earned enough money to invest in myself. I've been working out with a personal trainer at $150.00 a month. I'm looking pretty darn good after bearing two children, I must say. Now, I'm thinking of investing in a little Botox around the eyes and getting rid of these crow's feet. But, fear not. All my investments haven't been about me. I've even started an education fund for the kids. Their pre-paid tuition plan is paid in full, but additional expenses at college won't be covered. So, the education fund will be welcome when Kelly and Luke begin college.

Oh, and I tried the Huggies Cool Alerts for potty training Kelly. They worked like a charm. Makes me proud I invested in the company three years ago! For Luke, however, they'd have to put an electric shock in the damn things—he was tough.

Anyway, as a bond trader, Alan doesn't really understand stocks. I feel like the tables have turned. Remember when my eyes glazed over when he tried to tell me about bond trading? Well, he's been doing the same when I share my stock market info at the dinner table. He just pours himself another glass of expensive, '96 Mouton and asks about the kids, ignoring everything I've said. He's not acting like the finance wizard I used to know.

Now, I'm worried.

He's missed a couple of dinners this week. Told me he found a gym near his office and works out before coming home. Great stress reliever and a great idea. But, his breath reeks of alcohol when he comes through the door and kisses me.

He's either drinking on the train with his buddies, or stopping for drinks before coming home. Either way, his actions are hurting our family happiness. The kids end up in bed before he gets home, and he leaves before they're up in the morning. He's missing valuable family time. Yet, on the other hand, when he's with the kids he's an excellent father. We might have to re-think the merits of his commute for both his health and our home life.

I'm tempted to count the bottles in the wine cellar, but I just can't stoop that low. Nor will I nag Alan. He's a grown up. He's still loving and warm and makes love like a house on fire. If that aspect of our life begins to change, then I'll don the battle armor.

Meanwhile I'm trying to stay good looking, my frown lines are beginning to show and most of my friends have started to use Botox. I think it's time I tried it too, and besides I've done well enough with my investments to justify the cost—which isn't cheap. But, if I'm going to shoot the most lethal substance known to mankind into my forehead, I have to find the best!

Luckily for me, Emily introduced me to Dakota. Dakota's a fashion model. You've seen her on countless covers of fashion magazines. Yes, she's gorgeous, smart and really down-to-earth, and we've become great friends. She's also really great with her money and investments. She truly has it all! Anyway, Dakota recommended her cosmetic dermatologist who is so sought-after he wouldn't even see me without Dakota's referral. Did I hit pay dirt!

Dr. Beer's friendly, down-to-earth approach to beauty erased all my fears. I expressed my concerns about using Botox, but he explained them away.

Sounding oh, so technical, he said, *"Once injected, botulinum toxin is taken up by the nerves at the site of injection. After absorption, it blocks transmission of a chemical (acetylcholine) from a particular nerve to the muscle that it controls. Without this signal, the muscle relaxes and the wrinkle it caused begins to fade. No poisoning occurs during this procedure and no infection is possible, because the material is freeze dried powder. In other words, 'good-bye wrinkles'".*

"How long will it last?" I ventured to ask. *It's expensive stuff at about $350.00 per area. I calculate between my crow's feet and frown lines, that'll be two areas. $350.00 X 2 = $700.00. The price is still cheaper and less invasive than plastic surgery, but still.*

"Botox is not permanent because the nerves begin to sprout new connections to the muscle after a few months. The length varies between four and six months."

Dakota said, "Dr. Beer appears more expensive than the local 'botox party' that some of the girls go to, but rightly so. Botox is measured in units, not syringes - it is a freeze-dried powder that must be reconstituted before it can be injected. So, the 'Botox party' is selling a syringe of Botox at a discount. However, we never know the amount of units the syringe contains. Each bottle of Botox contains 100 units and each physician dilutes these 100 units differently. Many dermatologists use 2 cc of saline, others 4cc, and some as much as 10cc to dilute each bottle. Obviously, with 10cc of dilution the Botox won't work. I highly recommend avoiding Botox parties. Again, injecting products into your body should be done by a certified professional. Don't fool around with botulism!"

Anyway, after applying numbing cream to my forehead, Dr. Beer put the chair straight up and told me to squint. A few pin pricks later I was done! Relatively painless, I must say.

He told me to not exercise for the rest of the day. Do not lie down for the rest of the day (no problem with two children), and to work the product in by squinting and relaxing my forehead and eyes for the next couple of hours.

In four to seven days the Botox would kick in, and presto, the wrinkles would be gone. Alan would love this!

31

I would like to throttle Alan at the moment.

Valentine's Day should have been called Black Monday. Alan didn't even come home, seriously injuring our marital investment. He called at 9:30 pm saying he got stuck with some clients at a dinner, and it was too late to come home only to turn around and catch the early train in the morning.

Said he'd buy a new shirt, socks and underwear to get him through the next day.

I told him he was missing out on the best Valentine's Day of his life. I described this amazing Fredericks of Hollywood's number I'd bought that did incredible things to my cleavage. And I reminded him, the champagne was iced and waiting.

He said, "Oh, Sam. That's my favorite champagne. Don't drink it without me. We'll celebrate tomorrow night."

Damn. I'm madder than a Versace groupie forced to shop at K-Mart.

As I paced our bedroom in my negligee, drinking the freaking champagne without him—and yes, bore the hangover like a trooper the next morning—Alan's behavior got me thinking. Even though I'm thoroughly pleased with my small income from trading stocks, Kelly, Luke and I are dependent on Alan for our expenses. What if he gets too drunk and walks in front of a taxi, or falls in front of a train? (Yeah, I know. Dramatic.) But, you just can't be too careful nowadays and we have two kids. Alan puts himself out in that cold, cruel world every day. The pressures of his job, and heck, the commute to Manhattan alone could kill a man. Compound his high-pressure life with an inebriated state of mind and a girl's safe world could collapse with a phone call. Especially now that we have children, it was way past time to buy a life insurance policy. I decided black negligee and all, to check into it immediately!

I fired up the computer.

WHOLE LIFE - is purchased for the person's "whole" or entire life. This type of policy must be kept current and paid for the entire life of the insured. It is typically much more expensive than Term Life. There are several excellent reasons to purchase a 'whole life' policy, and some of them are to leave money to loved ones to pay bills, expenses and estate taxes. There is a cash value on this policy and it could pay dividends. The older you are when purchasing determines the amount of the premium, in other words Alan will pay a smaller amount at 40 than at 65 years old. If a parent has a 'whole life' policy a 'term life' policy would not be necessary unless he/she wanted additional insurance to help the children.

TERM LIFE is the simplest form of Life Insurance. This policy is for a specific amount of years, or a term, and will expire at the end of the designated time. It is designed for short range goals like extra insurance on parents of small children. And, the beauty is (if we can call insurance beautiful) is that large amounts can be purchased relatively inexpensively. Also, some companies will allow you to convert a Term Life policy into a Whole Life policy - for an additional premium of course!

I sat there reviewing the basic information on the Internet, and realized I'd have to call a professional insurance company to determine which policy would work for our situation. There are just so many different options—back to 'two minds working better than one'.

The next day, I called Alan after the market closed and managed to slide in a very quick question about it. *As it turns out, the company he works for offers Life and Disability Insurance for a small extra charge, and he had already taken out the maximum amount offered. The bad news is this coverage is only good as long as he works there. Should I kill him now, or wait a few weeks?*

Okay, things are getting worse. He didn't come home again, and while cleaning Alan's home office I discovered an application for a Home Equity Line of Credit. Now, I'm sure if Alan's planning to apply for a line of credit he will speak to me about it. But, something just isn't right. It's been three weeks and you'd think he had a new demanding job with the hours he's keeping. As you remember, trying to reach him on the trading floor is next to impossible, and I haven't been able to get through. But, I'm puzzled. We're pretty close to debt-free. So, why does Alan want a line of credit?

I'm going to do my homework and find out exactly what a Home Equity Line of Credit means to our financial situation. Back to the computer!

HOME EQUITY LINES OF CREDIT

By using the equity (value of home minus the outstanding mortgage) in our home, we can apply for a line of credit. In other words, the bank would set-up a loan of available money from which we can draw when and however we want. Our home would be used as collateral. This means, we can borrow the money up to the allotted amount, but if we don't pay them back on time, with interest, our home could become the lenders/banks.

Once again, a home equity line of credit gives you access to a set amount of money, and your 'home' is used to guarantee the loan. The fees to set-up the line of credit can be high, so most homeowners only use it for large purchases like college tuition, home improvements and medical bills. Typically, home equity lines of credit are structured on variable interest rates.

The fees are structured just like a normal loan, and usually involve:
- *An appraisal to determine the value of your home*
- *Application fee*

- *Up-front charges*
- *Closing costs including fees for attorneys, title search, mortgage preparation and filing*
- *Property and title insurance*
- *Taxes.*

I've also learned about second mortgage loans, which are similar to lines of credit. A second mortgage provides a fixed amount of money repayable over a fixed period of time, and typically has a set interest rate.

An excellent website that lists the pros and cons of a home equity line of credit is www.federalreserve.gov. Take a moment to visit this site.

The good news is that the interest on a Home Equity Line of Credit will probably be deductible from our taxes. And, we could pay off any outstanding bills, or future purchases with the money—but, we don't have any outstanding bills. I have specifically paid bills on time and kept us out of debt because I would hate to lose the home my children live in because of bad debt, and I want to keep our credit rating high. So, why would we want more debt if we didn't have to? The words from the government website, "**THE TRANSACTION PUTS YOUR HOME AT RISK**", kept ringing in my ears.

With Alan not coming home for Valentine's Day, and finding this application for a line of credit, my antennae came on full alert. I'm still not sure why Alan wants this line of credit, maybe he wants to build a pool—in which case a second mortgage might be a better plan. But, I'll bet it has to do with the wine collection, because the line of credit would provide cash flow only if he needs it.

Okay, time's up. We need to have a serious couple's financial conversation about what he's planning for our money.

32

O h, gawd. Alan's been fired! That's the reason for the line of
credit.

Remember when he told me that one mistake can cost a bond
trader his job? Well, Alan made three. *He's been trading proprietary
asset-backed securities (in other words, a billion US dollars of credit card
assets for the firm) and got on the wrong side of the trade and lost the firm
an enormous amount of money.* What's worse—it was his idea and he
had convinced the CEO to go along.

Alan's high enough on the totem pole that they permitted him
three errors, but now they've farmed him out. He was fired on
Valentine's Day and drank himself into a stupor. Bad enough. Yes?

No.

I found pink lipstick on the collar of the dirty shirt he brought
home. Alan was probably too drunk to notice and destroy the
evidence.

And, to compound the bad news ... the wine cellar is almost
empty. While I may be guilty of snitching a bottle here and there (but
recorded each removal on the inventory list), Alan has been drinking
the stock into extinction!

Our wine investment has been marinating his liver! My marriage
is in deep doo-doo and I'm a wreck.

I've been crying for two weeks. He looked completely confused when I showed him the lipstick stain. I mean, completely confused. I told him no more sex for us until he goes for an STD/AIDS test. If he's picking up bimbos, he's not bringing any bugs home to me! And I put a padlock on the wine cellar.

Nobody but nobody knows where the key is ... except me.

Emily says I should divorce his sexy ass. (Her words.) I just can't do that. We need marriage counseling. He's too precious to lose.

The bastard!

While I gathered my wits about me, I threw Alan out for a couple of days. We both needed time to let the enormity of the situation sink in.

Within a week, we met for a pow-wow. Alan announced he'd found a job working at a Hedge Fund (whatever the hell that is!) in Darien. He's convinced working close to home will help stabilize his life. He says he misses the kids and working locally will give them more time together. So far, so good. He's been truly contrite and begged for my forgiveness.

I caved. He's home, and on his best behavior.

Still, finance addict that I am, the words "hedge fund" kept nudging me. So, to break the icy air the dinner table, I asked Alan to explain a hedge fund to us (it was pure joy watching a grown man explain a hedge fund to a five year old). The poor guy. He jumped at the opportunity to speak civilly with me after the wrath I've been unleashing upon him. He said, *"Honey, the best way to explain a hedge fund is to start from the beginning again. There are basically four (4) things you can do with your money. One, buy something—stocks or equity. Two, loan your money—bonds or debt. Three, invest in commodities like orange juice, oil, currencies, metals, etc. And four, keep it in cash—money market funds, CD's etc. Every other type of trade, like options or futures for example, is derived from one of these four things—Wall Street calls all these other types of trades 'derivatives'. A 'hedge fund' uses derivatives to protect your money by placing trades to ensure that if the market turns against you, you will be protected, i.e. a 'hedge'."*

"In my new position at the Hedge Fund, I'll be trading bond futures and derivatives. Therefore, I'll be ensuring my clients make the most money possible, but are protected if the market goes down. And, the best part: I make one percent of the monies invested and 20% of the profit."

Memories of Christopher Steinberg crept into my mind. Jeeze, maybe we'll be rolling in dough soon!

Alan looked at me with those big baby blue eyes, hoping to get invited back to our bed. He knew that appealing to the financial addict in me was like an aphrodisiac. But that volcano of distrust still fumed inside. Alan had crossed the trust boundary and that's a hard one to recover.

The next morning, at a loss with my emotions, I called Morgan. My rock. My voice of reason. After promising to roast his private parts next to Keith's, she calmed down.

"Oh, Sam. Alan is the love of your life. For better or worse, remember? I know you two can get through this mess."

She dredged up good times from the past to remind me of the great life Alan and I had built. She was firm in the belief that cheating was inexcusable, but a fact of life. If Alan was truly remorseful, we had too much invested in our relationship to throw it all away so fast. As wise as she is, and as much as I didn't want to hear it, she believed that if Alan and I could get over this hurdle, time would be the true healer.

We discussed the facts, including the needs of the children. Then, we returned to finances. After about twenty minutes, she made one financial point clearer than day: *It would be better to hang on to my marriage for at least ten (10) years. Judges don't view ten years as a magic number as they always review the facts, but longer marriages have a different psychological impact than shorter marriages. With ten years under my belt, I will at least deserve part of his Social Security, and I do have a pre-nup, but the children couldn't be part of it because they didn't exist.* This is good information to tuck away, but it was the last fact I'd want to use.

Truth was: I wanted to save my marriage.

Alan was and always will be my first love. Life's been giving him a run for his money, as the saying goes. Alcoholism is a monster, but he can beat it. He says he wants to. And, most important, Alan says he still loves me. I believe him, but I'm steaming mad. His STD tests were clean, and we always had a great love life, so our make-up sex fell into the, "fuck you asshole, I love you" kind. I was someplace between strangling him and wanting to throw him against the wall. Actually, it was sexy and kinky beyond my usual bounds. I'll have to try more of this as my fortieth birthday stares me in the eye.

It's just around the corner. I'm prepared to count my blessings. We have two beautiful kids. More precious than gold. Kelly's ready to start kindergarten and Luke is right on her heels. They still climb all over Daddy, oblivious to the battle raging between us.

So, I made my decision.

I'm going to love this guy, even though it hurts. We scheduled our first marriage counseling for this Thursday. I need my man back. Our kids need their Daddy. I'm going to give Alan all the love I have. Hopefully, by our tenth anniversary, our love will be blossoming again.

I can already see that turning forty has brought me greater wisdom, and investing in my marriage makes good emotional and financial sense. Like I said, I'll never quit my finance addiction. It's as necessary as love. I told you that from the very beginning. I'll keep telling you that until the very end.

"BONDS HAVE MORE FUN"

With her marriage on the rocks, Samantha Davis-Abercrombie focuses all her energy on repairing her relationship while continuing to raise two children, and scrambling to seal a cracked nest egg. Throughout it all, our girl remains unstoppable. She delves back into the work force, starts her own business, and hires an advisor to help manage her funds.

Shocked by how fast time is passing, before she can trade her Dolce and Gabbana bag for a newer model, the kids are already heading off to college. Luckily for Sam, her coffers are finally brimming. With the kids away, Sam decides it's time for a personal overhaul—after all, not only will she feel wonderful, but a few fillers and tucks will perk up her drooping sex life. (It's hell to admit the truth!) Of course, she doesn't make a move without consulting dermatologists and personal trainers. In no time at all, not only does she look fabulous, but soon finds love in the most interesting places. (Is it with her husband? You'll have to read on to find out!)

Jimmy Choos strapped on, Samantha tangos' through love and finance with grace and, um … well, slipping on the occasional banana peel, but that's life and learning finance with Samantha Davis-Abercrombie. Grab your sparkling water, latte or Chardonnay and read on while Samantha entertains you with sound financial advice and outrageous love in the next book: *"BONDS HAVE MORE FUN!"*

About the Authors

*G*wendolyn Beck has a Series 65, NASD Uniform Investment Adviser Law; and had a Series 7, Securities and Exchange Commission (SEC) Registered Representative Exam; Series 63, National Association of Securities Dealers (NASD) Uniform Securities Agent State Law Exam; and Series 31, National Futures Managed Funds. She also had a Florida Real Estate license and had a Florida Life Insurance & Variable Annuity License.

She went to Florida State University (go Noles) and received a Bachelor of Science in International Affairs. Before FSU, she received an Associate of Arts from Brevard Community College, and has taken graduate courses at both FSU and George Washington University. While working at Credit Suisse, she studied finance at the New York Institute of Finance.

At Morgan Stanley, she successfully completed their Wharton School series on Estate Planning, Financial Planning, Women and Investing, Lump Sum Distribution and Retirement Planning, and Asset Allocation: Strategic Wealth Building.

*K*athleen Pickering, who has made this book so much fun, will have you laughing, crying and anxious to see what happens to Samantha next! She was the President of the Florida Romance Writers of America, has won numerous awards including the Maggie Award and the Holt Medallion Award. She is the author of Harlequin Super Romance,

189

"Where It Began", "Echoes of Love", "Mythological Sam", "Vampires, Werewolves & Zombies, Oh My!", and founder of the Mega-Author's Visionary Club. And, has several Harlequin Super Romance novels in the works.

Together, they make learning about finance fun, easy and exciting! Only thing better than that is finding your favorite shoes on sale. Enjoy!

APPENDIX A

M ost checking accounts will come with coded checks. This will be immensely helpful in keeping track of your money going out. Try to get an account that sends you a year end statement. This will help you keep a handle on all of your money.

The codes will generally look like this:

CODE	CATEGORY	CODE	CATEGORY
A	ACCOUNTING/LEGAL	N	SERVICES/LABOR
B	BUSINESS	O	SUPPLIES
C	CONTRIBUTIONS/DONATIONS	P	CLOTHING
D	DUES/SUBSCRIPTIONS	Q	DEPENDENT CARE
E	EDUCATION	R	REPAIRS
F	FOOD/GROCERIES	T	TRAVEL
G	RENT/MORTGAGE	U	UTILITIES
H	LOANS/CREDIT CARDS	V	CAR/TRANSPORTATION
J	INSURANCE—1	W	TAXES—FEDERAL
K	INSURANCE—2	X	TAXES—STATE
M	MEDICAL/DENTAL	Y	TAXES—MISC

There should also be a space for your own categories. I would recommend designating one for manicures/pedicures and any other personal spa services that you regularly use.

This is how a checking account works:

1. You deposit money into the account.
2. The bank or investment house holds your money.
3. When you write a check or use your debit card the amount is taken from your checking account and paid to the retailer and/or person you gave the money to.
4. Be sure not to exceed the amount you have deposited into the account, or your check will 'bounce'. If your check 'bounces' there is a substantial fee associated with this!
5. Avoid all fees if possible!

APPENDIX B
WHAT ALAN DOES:
HOW THE U.S. GOVERNMENT
SECURITIES MARKETS WORK

***Remember, this is really important if you ever get into real estate, buy real estate or meet a hot bond trader!

The Federal Government watches the economy to determine how to pace interest rates. The Government will either put money into the economy (loosen/lower interest rates) or take money out of the economy (tighten/raise interest rates). They do this by adjusting the Discount Rate and the Federal Funds rate. The Discount Rate is the rate the Federal Reserve, our country's central bank, offers for loans to member banks. The Federal Funds rate is the rate that banks use to lend money to each other. The Fed Funds rate is the U.S. short-term benchmark. The Fed Funds rate influences market interest rates throughout the world.

Okay, this is a bit complicated, but flows nicely through your system, once you get the hang of it. I'll teach you how to trade bonds in the next book, "Bonds Have More Fun", but for now here's an overview of how it all works.

1. The Federal Reserve's Federal Open Market Committee (FOMC) meets to discuss interest rates. They raise or lower the rates depending on the state of the economy. The state of the economy is based on economic data that is gathered by various governmental and private organizations, and released throughout the month. (We will cover this in detail in "Bonds Have More Fun"). The most important of this data is the employment figures which is released at 8:30am EST on the first Friday of the month (turn on CNBC and watch the excitement).

2. 2. The FOMC will meet every six weeks to discuss interest rates and the state of the economy. They will usually announce at 2:15 p.m. if there will be a change in rates, however they can change rates at any time unexpectedly. If you are going to lock in a mortgage, be sure to check the newspaper's financial or business section to see what the trend in interest rates is and what the experts are saying about the direction of rates. You could save a lot of money by acting quickly or waiting, depending on what direction the rates are taking.

3. 3. US Government Securities are traded at 39 US Investment Banks such as JP Morgan, Credit Suisse, Morgan Stanley, and Merrill Lynch. These banks have to be authorized to trade. (There were 40 banks until Kidder Peabody went under because of a rogue bond trader.) Alan works at Credit Suisse First Boston.

4. 4. These investment banks buy newly issued US Government Securities directly from the government through an auction format. These securities are referred to as 'on-the-run' until the next new issued comes out. Once the next new issue comes out, they are called 'off-the-run' and traded freely in the market place. This might confuse you, but just think of buying something new versus buying something used which has great market value (like an heirloom diamond or that little, white Louis Vuitton bag that had a waiting list of 800 at the stores a couple of years ago).

5. 5. One US Government Security (5 and 10 year notes, and 30 year bond) is worth $1000. [Note: Securities are blocked into different years because you may want the money back in different years. If you're retired you'll want your money at 65, 66, 67, 68 etc.] These Securities will pay a set amount of interest (let's say 5% for our example). Now, once these securities hit the open market by being released to trading/investment houses like Schwab, Morgan Stanley, etc. and trade freely, it will raise or lower in price, and the yield, which has an inverse relationship (opposite), will go the other way. For example, if the price goes down to $950 there will be a 5.5% yield. If the price goes up $1050, there will be a 4.5% yield. There is also a zero-coupon bond, which has no yield, trades for less, and matures at $1000. The benefit of a zero-coupon bond is that the interest accrues so you don't get money every year, but get full value when it matures. This is great if you don't need current income. For example, retirement or college saving strategies could have zero coupon bonds that will mature when you turn 65, 66, 67, etc, or when you get to college at 17, 18, 19, etc. You can only buy out 30 years.

6. Depending on the state of the economy, and what the FOMC does, determines if the price of bonds goes up or goes down. Think of your parent's mortgage and what interest rate they pay. It's all determined on the above items—knowledge of this will also be important for your mortgage payments. Bond traders make very sophisticated predictions on whether the price will move up or move down. They used extremely complex mathematical calculations and computers to determine price and yield movements. An enormous amount of money is at stake with these calculations. That is why Alan is only allowed one mistake in his career.

So, when Alan had his bad day, it was as if he took your money to invest in a hot, new pointy-toe Manolo Blahniks, only to discover suddenly that everyone was wearing round toe Pradas. He'd start yelling SELL, SELL, SELL to get rid of the outdated shoes he bought with your money in order to buy the newer ones. Meanwhile, no one wants to buy your old shoes, so the price is going down on the Manolo's and the prices are rapidly rising on the Pradas. Apply this to invested money and clearly you have a disaster of phenomenal proportions!

INDEX